£2

STEP BY STEP ART SCHOOL
CERAMICS

GERALDINE CHRISTY
AND SARA PEARCH

HAMLYN

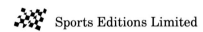 Sports Editions Limited

Managing Director	Richard Dewing
Art Director	Mary Hamlyn
Senior Designer	Rob Kelland
Designer	Sandra Cowell
Design Assistant	Lyndon Brooks
Editor	Leslie Smillie
Editorial Assistant	Joanna Mawson

This edition first published 1992
Hamlyn is an imprint of Octopus Illustrated Publishing
Michelin House, 81 Fulham Road, London SW3 6RB
part of Reed International Books

A catalogue record for this book is available from the British Library.

ISBN 0 600 57546 2

Designed and edited by
Sports Editions Limited
3 Greenlea Park
Prince George's Road
London
SW19 2JD

Produced by Mandarin Offset
Printed in Hong Kong

Contents

Chapter 1

Introduction

Popular interest in ceramics has been growing steadily, and with good reason. Ceramics has something for everyone — as a craft it provides the opportunity to make a wide range of functional items, and as an art it offers a form of self-expression with infinite combinations of colour and texture.

This book introduces a number of techniques and ideas for decoration in the form of projects. It is hoped that they provide a springboard into working with and enjoying the medium of clay. The methods outlined have been tried and tested, but many potters have individual ways of approaching their work, and if you discover another technique that works well for you, then go ahead and use it. In the same way, the sections on decoration are meant to be a guide, and perhaps they will give you some inspiration towards developing your own personal style. There are no real rules in pottery other than technical ones, and many of those are broken by established potters, so if the result is satisfying then you have succeeded.

The first chapter looks at the history of ceramics and illustrates some of the artistry of potters working today.

Introduction

THE CERAMICS TRADITION

The discovery that clay baked to a hardness could be used as a method of constructing containers for food and liquids must surely have been a breakthrough in human progress. Early pots were hand built, often from coils, and simply baked in a fire or just left to dry in the sun. Yet by 4000 BC surviving Egyptian pottery shows refinement of shape and decoration.

With the invention of the potter's wheel, working with clay began to develop into a craft of immense ingenuity, variety and expression. Fine ceramic art was a feature of the Classical Greek period, and the Chinese, too, were developing a strong tradition of ceramics early in their history, producing stoneware pots and sculptured figures and animals with colourful lead-based glazes, most notably the green celadon glaze. By the time of the T'ang dynasty (7th to 10th century) they had perfected the technique of producing fine porcelain, which was to have a major influence on European ceramics from the 16th century onwards.

Islamic craftsmen took in the ideas that the Chinese could offer in the form of brilliant glazes, developing their own distinctive cultural tradition, particularly in the specialist area of tiles, and introducing a sophisticated calligraphic style. They also developed decorative techniques using tin glazes and lustre, which gave an attractive metallic finish. These innovations passed to Spain, then Italy, and by the time of the Renaissance, European potters were benefitting from the wealth of ceramic art produced by the Eastern civilizations.

As tin-glazing techniques were perfected in the 16th and 17th centuries a European tradition developed producing pottery in vibrant colours, known as faience in France, majolica in Italy and Delft in the Netherlands. Dutch ceramic ware, particularly

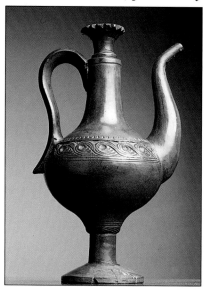

Traditional North African rose-water ewer, made of earthenware, incised and burnished.

in the manufacture of tiles, was strongly influenced by the blue and white porcelain which was being exported in large quantities from China.

European potteries worked hard to achieve the translucent quality of porcelain that Chinese potters had produced for centuries, and a pottery was set up at Sèvres to manufacture imitation soft-paste porcelain. It was not until the early 18th century, however, that factories making hard-paste porcelain developed in Europe. The great 'china' factories of Meissen, Chelsea, Bow and Derby were

established at around this time. By the mid-18th century Josiah Wedgwood had set up his pottery in Staffordshire, England, and was soon producing 'creamware', an earthenware which was to become more popular than tin-glazed pottery, and later 'jasperware' in the familiar matt colours with which his name is associated.

Throughout the Victorian period, in an age of industrialization and mass-production, fine 'china' was readily available but there was little individual manufacture of great note. Towards the end of the 19th century, however, there was a flourishing of artist-craftsmen, strongly influenced by the Art and Crafts movement and working in the Art Nouveau style, who injected a new vitality into ceramics, particularly in the matter of form and decoration.

The revival of the 'studio' potter in the 20th century owes much to one individual — Bernard Leach, who travelled to Japan, and learned the traditional techniques, returning to establish his own pottery in England in 1920. Many glaze recipes were collected and developed by Leach, and much of the ethos of the potter's studio, methods and tools used have been directly influenced by the Japanese.

Today, age-old tradition has combined with the enthusiasm and benefits of the technological era, opening ceramics into an exciting art with endless possibilities. Artist-potters with individual styles are thriving and producing a constant stream of wonderful pots.

John Maltby
Stoneware vase, slab built
in two sections (body and
neck). The body is
decorated with coloured
clays and slips. The neck
has a black stoneware
glaze.

Lucie Rie
Stoneware vase thrown in
sections, with a stunning
spiral twist from top to
bottom, by one of the
world's finest potters.

Janet Leach
Taking its inspiration from
Japanese Bizen ware, this
stoneware pot has ash
glaze marks produced by
straw in the wood-fired
kiln.

Japanese potter

An Unomi tea bowl made in stoneware. The pot is hand thrown and turned, and has an onglaze decoration of maple leaves. Not only are many of the forms of Japanese pots traditional, particularly for the ritual tea ceremony, but so are the methods of working. Wooden tools, many of which are hand made, are preferred for their sympathy to the clay, and Japanese potters are apprenticed for some time to a 'master' potter.

Lucie Rie

This stoneware bowl displays a subtle twist of purple around its base, its colour and texture perfectly complementing the form. Lucie Rie has spent a lifetime experimenting with glazes and her effects are achieved by the body of the clay reacting with the glaze rather than by adding decoration. The outside of a bowl is glazed first and left to dry before glazing the inside and she takes great care in the finish of her pots, making sure that the line around the foot is neat. Lucie Rie fires her pots slowly, reaching 1250°C (2280°F).

Christine-Ann Richards

Many potters have devised their own methods for producing striking effects. The superb green glaze used for this porcelain bowl contains 8 per cent copper carbonate. The crackle is achieved by taking the pot out of the kiln at 300°C (570°F) and sprinkling water on it. Black ink is then brushed into the crazing and as the pot cools this seeps into the cracks. The ink is washed off the surface when the pot is cool, within 24 hours. Prior to this the pot is biscuit fired at 800-900°C (1470-1650°F). The final firing is to 1260-1290°C (2300-2350°F). The shape of the foot is produced by skimming with a metal tool.

Sara Pearch

This saki pot is a traditional form known as Sueki, and dates back 800 years. The pot is coiled and thrown in four sections, then fired in a wood-fired kiln.

Margaret MacEvoy
Salt-glazed bottle, thrown in stoneware clay. The soft smoky pinks, greys and amber are produced by firing the pot in a saggar, a clay container, inside the kiln. A saggar protects the pot from direct flame in a fuel-burning kiln without a purpose-built inner chamber.

Anna Noel
Tiger modelled in raku and fired to 1000°C (1830°F), then finally reduced. A rich yellow glaze is used for the yellow stripes, while the black is natural clay which has been reduced to produce a dark smoky colour. The body of the tiger is not solid, but has a hole underneath to stop the pot exploding in the kiln.

Antonia Salmon
Stoneware pot, hand built from slabs. The pot was fired in a sawdust wood-fired kiln and was fired at biscuit stage at slightly over 980°C (1800°F). Before first firing the pot was meticulously smoothed with a metal spoon, producing a beautiful burnished sheen. Finally it was waxed to retain the soft colouring produced by the wood smoke.

Portuguese potter
Traditional earthenware
water ewer with a pulled
handle and a spout to
drink from. The subtle
colouring is achieved by
firing in a wood-fired kiln
with nut shells.

Adidal Abou-chamat
Hand-thrown raku pot
with a small hole. Fired in
a raku kiln at 1000°C
(1830°F), the green
blushes are produced by
copper carbonate. After
removing it from the kiln
the pot was reduced in
sawdust.

Clive Bowen
Red earthenware jug
decorated with slip
applied with a slip trailer.
The black slip is produced
by adding manganese and
the yellow slip contains
iron. Bold decoration is
suited to such a strong
form and the various
parts of the jug are well
defined. The jug was fired
in a wood-burning kiln.

Pat Fuller
Stoneware bottle fired in a salt-glaze kiln. Salt glaze produces an attractive lightly speckled effect and is achieved by the reaction of the salt with coloured slip or stain. Great care is needed in salt glazing as harmful fumes are given off. The sgraffito decoration on the bottle was done with a piece of wood.

Geoffrey Fuller
Earthenware bottle, slipped and decorated with a clear glaze with oxide. There is a sprig decoration on the shoulder. This thrown bottle is squared off with a flat piece of wood.

John Leach
Stoneware pot fired in a wood-fired kiln. The ash glaze flows over the shoulder of the pot, providing a contrast to the balance of the form and the matt texture of the body. The curve of the handle and top of the pot echo the curved walls.

Chapter 2

Tools and equipment

The vast array of tools available for use in ceramics may seem rather daunting to the beginner. There are so many different types that can be used in throwing, shaping and modelling and it is a matter of personal preference as to which may be the most suitable for the sort of pots you intend to make. Choose tools that are comfortable to hold, and only buy them as you need them. You can make many tools for yourself or improvise with kitchen utensils.

As far as basic equipment is concerned the only piece that is absolutely necessary is a kiln, and, of course, if you want to work on techniques more advanced than slab or coil pottery, you will need a wheel.

If you are lucky enough to have the space why not set up your own studio? Try to organize your tools and tasks so that each has its own allotted working area.

The most important material, however, is the clay itself. If you are starting from scratch try out the different clays before you decide to specialize. They all vary slightly in feel and familiarizing yourself with them will give you confidence in ceramics.

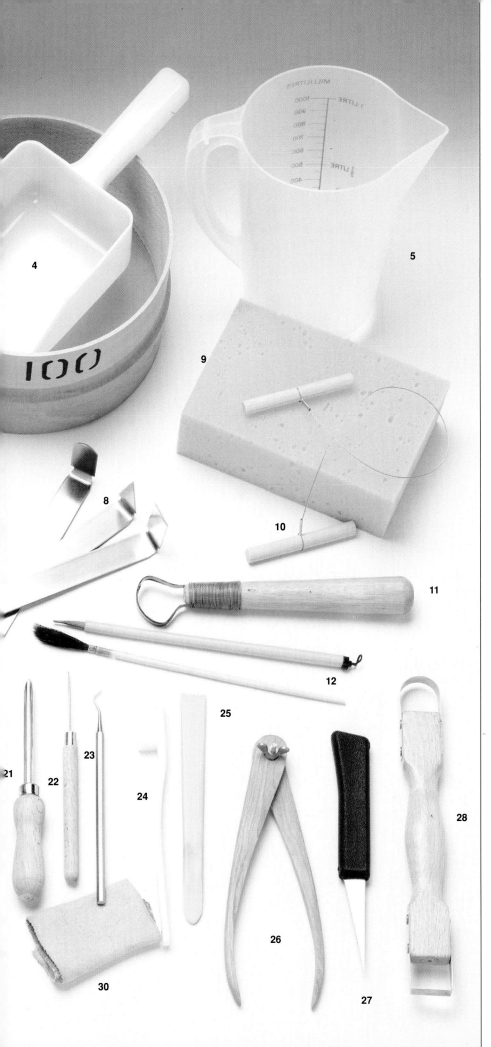

BASIC TOOLS

1 Gauntlets for removing pots from the kiln.

2 Calipers for accurate measuring of large pots.

3 Sieves for slips and glazes. Available in several mesh sizes.

4 Plastic scoop for powdered clay and glaze materials.

5 Measuring jug for adding water to slips and glazes.

6 Rolling pin for rolling out clay.

7 Slip trailer for decoration.

8 Metal turning tools.

9 Sponge for cleaning tools.

10 Cheesewire for cutting pot from wheel.

11 Loop tool for hollowing out or for turning large pots.

12 Brushes of varying widths.

13 Slip or glaze brush (flat hake brush) for applying slip or glaze.

14 Wooden throwing ribs.

15 Metal and rubber kidneys, or credit card — all useful for smoothing and shaping.

16 Bamboo turning tool.

17 Small natural sponge for throwing, smoothing and cleaning pots.

18 Glaze mop for painting glaze on to pots.

19 Bamboo tool with string for making lids from a hump of clay.

20 Wooden modelling tool for fluting.

21 Hole cutter for making holes.

22 Potter's pin for cutting and incising.

23 Dentist's tool for modelling.

24 Toothbrush for flicking colour on or preparing clay for joining.

25 Wooden modelling tool for shaping or decoration.

26 Calipers for accurate measuring of small pots.

27 Potter's knife.

28 Double loop tool for hollowing out or turning large pots.

29 Throwing hook for bellying pots.

30 Chamois leather for smoothing, particularly rims.

19

Keeping a special working place for ceramics makes the whole business of working with clay much easier. With everything in its place you can organize your work properly and if you have room for a small studio so much the better.

Wherever you work it is important to have a good light source. If possible this should be provided by natural light as it is much less tiring on the eyes, but do provide the best possible electric lighting for use when necessary.

If you are planning a studio from scratch decide on the position of electrical sockets first so that you can site your kiln and wheel. Even if you do not have an electric kiln and use a kick wheel it is worth catering for the possibility that you might change your equipment in the future. The kiln should be placed where it is not likely to be in the way, and where its heat will not cause any damage. Keep a fire extinguisher nearby as a precaution — if a fire should start you need to put it out as quickly as possible. Also position an extractor fan near the kiln to remove any toxic fumes given off during the firing process.

The wheel also needs to be well sited. Try to keep it to one side of the room as near to the light as possible and out of the way of doors so that there is no possibility of being knocked while you are working.

If it is possible to have running water this is a great asset, as you need to keep the clay wet as you work. Clay can also be extremely messy, and it is important to keep your tools and equipment clean. A double-draining sink is the ideal, with one sink draining into another underneath. Sludge and waste pieces of clay sink to the bottom while the water flows away. You will have to clean out the bottom sink every so often.

The main preparation area should be easily accessible, and if you can position this in the middle of the room so much the better. Keep all your tools together, each with a place of its own so that you can put your hand on something as soon as you need it. Wedge your clay here — a marble slab is best for this — and keep your clay bins nearby. You should have two bins for clay, one for the storage of new clay and another into which left-over pieces can be put for recycling by wedging. Wet, prepared clay that you are about to use should be placed on a marble slab, with your scales to hand to weigh the precise amount for each pot.

Mix up fairly large quantities of slip and glaze so that it is ready when you need it, and enough to cover the whole pot when dipped in. Keep the bins near the preparation area, but with sufficient floor space around to

give you room when preparing the mixtures. Make sure that small containers of coloured slip and glazes are clearly labelled.

One item that you will find most useful is a damp box or cupboard. This will allow you to store half-finished pots overnight and prevent them from drying out. Simply spray water into the box or cupboard before placing the pot inside. This is also helpful if you are working on a number of pots in one session and need to leave any for a length of time.

Any spare wall space should be taken up with shelving. Newly

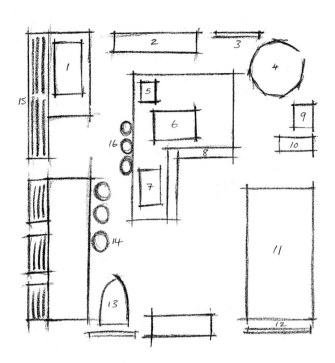

thrown, slipped or decorated pots may have to dry out on a shelf for a while. As they are fragile at all stages of their making it is advisable to use removable boards as shelves. The whole shelf can be moved without actually having to touch the pots and risk any damage. You will also need shelves to put your finished pots on. If you are hoping to sell your ceramics from your studio then a tidy and attractive display of wares is essential. If you are making pots for your own pleasure it is good to have the satisfaction of looking at your finished work.

Lastly, try to leave enough space for a pinboard on your wall. Not only will it be useful for notes reminding yourself of routine tasks such as materials to be bought and kiln firing times, but it also provides a place for pictures and postcards of anything that might inspire you.

Plan of typical studio

1 Sink.
2 Damp cupboard or box.
3 Pinboard.
4 Kiln.
5 Scales.
6 Marble slab for wedging.
7 Tools.
8 Extractor fan.
9 Fire extinguisher.
10 Display area.
11 Windows.
12 Wheel.
13 Bins for slip and glazes.
14 Adjustable shelving with loose boards.
15 Clay bins for recycling old clay and storage of new clay.

TIPS AND HINTS

Make sure that the clay is never contaminated with plaster — it will explode in the kiln.

CLAY

There is an almost irresistible urge when you see a piece of clay to take it in your hands and to shape it into some form or other. It is the plasticity of clay that attracts so many people to the craft of ceramics. Perhaps it also jogs a primitive memory, a basic recognition that clay comes from the earth, and brings into play the age-old battle between man and the forces of nature.

Clay is formed by the decomposition of rock, and in geological terms is classified into two groups — primary or residual, and secondary or sedimentary. Primary clays are found in the area in which they formed and are not very plastic in their natural state. They can, however, be added to other clays for making pottery. Most pottery clays are composed of sedimentary bodies that have been carried away from their place of formation. In moving they have been refined, becoming plastic in the process. They have also taken in impurities such as oxides and minerals which change their colour and properties.

In the preparation of clay for pottery further minerals may be added and clays may be combined together to improve the quality. Grog, or sand particles, may also be added to change the texture. You can prepare your own clay by buying the ingredients in powdered form to mix with water, but beginners will find, as do many established potters, that commercially prepared clay is more consistent and less trouble.

There are four basic types of clay that are used in pottery — earthenware, stoneware, porcelain and raku — and many varieties within these types. Each has different properties and fires to a different temperature. To a great extent the clay you work with depends on personal choice, but because of the specific firing temperatures required, the main deciding factor is the kind of kiln you use. If you have any queries do not hesitate to ask the advice of your potter's supplier. Look after your clay — store it carefully in a damp environment to prevent it drying out and save any left-over in a bin to be used later.

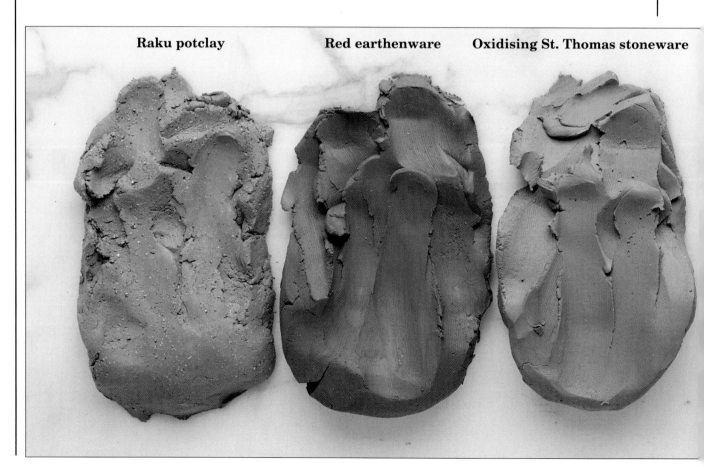

Raku potclay   **Red earthenware**   **Oxidising St. Thomas stoneware**

Earthenware

Although it is generally thought of as a red clay, earthenware is also available in white or buff, based on a fine ball clay, one of the refined sedimentary group of clays. It has traditionally been used for domestic items and has been used for the majority of pots in the projects in this book. Earthenware can be fired in any kind of kiln. Biscuit fire at 1000°C (1830°F). Glaze fire at 1040-1160°C (1900-2120°F).

Stoneware

Stoneware must be fired to a high temperature and produces a stronger, heavier pot than earthenware. Subtle effects can be produced in stoneware when it is reduction fired and for this reason it is advisable to use a gas-fired kiln so that the power can be reduced quickly or switched off. Biscuit fire at 1000°C (1830°F). Glaze fire at 1200-1300°C (2190-2370°F).

Porcelain

Historically recognized as an extremely fine clay, porcelain has a hard, almost glass-like finish when fired as the glaze fuses with the body of the clay. Generally white or pale in colour, it has qualities of translucence that are not found in other clays, but it can also be opaque. Porcelain becomes wet very quickly and the particles in the clay continue to 'move' when thrown, so experience is required in handling it to greatest effect. Biscuit fire at 1000°C (1830°F). Glaze fire at 1240-1300°C (2260-2370°F).

Raku

Raku is a coarse-grained clay that contains a lot of grog or sand particles. It produces a textured finish and is most suitable for rounded decorative forms. Firing at a lower temperature than other clays, raku can be returned to the kiln several times using reduction and oxidation methods until a pleasing result is achieved. Its unpredictability can give some surprisingly stunning effects. Biscuit fire at 900°C (1650°F). Glaze fire at 800-1000°C (1470-1830°F).

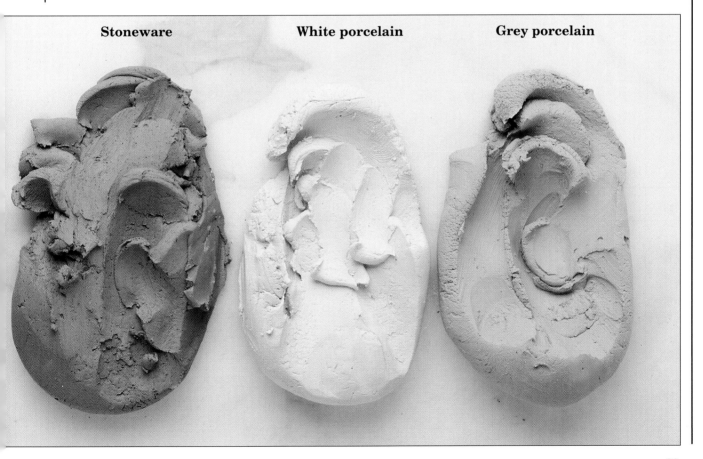

Stoneware   White porcelain   Grey porcelain

Chapter 3
Essential techniques

Many methods in ceramics are a matter of finding the way of working that best suits you, but there are certain techniques that are essential to successful potting. These include preparing the actual clay, taking care in applying slip to your pot, and diligently overseeing the firing processes.

In order to work with clay of an even and pliable consistency you must knead it well, pushing out all the air in the process. You may find it useful to prepare enough clay for the day's work or session, storing it in a damp box or wrapped in a damp towel to keep it from drying out.

Many decorative techniques involve the application of slip, a mixture of clay and water, which can be coloured to produce a variety of effects.

Mixing slip by hand is a long and sometimes tiring job, but it is important to make it smooth so that your decoration is even.

The final process in the story of a pot is its firing. Choosing the right kiln for the type of clay you are using, understanding the kiln's capabilities and the problems of biscuit and glaze firing are all essential in achieving a pleasing result.

Essential techniques

WEDGING CLAY

Good preparation is important at all stages of making a pot. It is essential when preparing the clay itself, for a pot that is made from poorly prepared clay is difficult to work. More serious than this is the fact that it may crack, or even shatter, in the kiln during the firing process. This can be heartbreaking when you have put a good deal of time, effort and imagination into your pottery. A main culprit in a possible series of disasters is air trapped in bubbles in the clay — and the way to eliminate the problem is to knead the clay carefully and thoroughly. By pushing out the air from the clay you also achieve a pliable and consistent material with which to work.

The initial process for kneading is known as 'wedging'. Large blocks of clay can be sliced into manageable pieces, then pressed and folded together to make them softer. The kneading process involves turning and rolling the clay in a special movement. There are many methods of wedging and kneading, and you can adapt the method shown here to your own individual way of working.

After patting the clay into a 'log' for slicing into appropriate amounts it can be stored in a damp box for future use.

1 A large block of clay is difficult to work, so smaller pieces can be prepared by 'wedging' and kneading to remove any air bubbles. Cut off slices with a cheesewire.

2 At this stage the clay might be quite hard, so to soften it press down into the slice with your knuckles. Do this as much as is necessary to really break up the surface of the slice and make it pliable. Make sure that the table is clean throughout the whole process of wedging, so that the clay does not stick.

3 If you have some spare bits of clay left over from previous pottery sessions you can water this down into a slurry and add it to the slice of clay. Squeeze and push it well into the indentations, pressing down with your knuckles so that the soft clay is well mixed in. Hard clay is difficult to work and has less flexibility so it is worth putting some effort into this process.

4 Now add another slice of clay, and press down again into it with your knuckles to join the layers together. While you are adding and pushing clay down you will be able to hear bubbles of air bursting. Wedging may seem rather hard work, but it is an ideal way to get a feel for clay.

26

5 With what is basically still a square shape of clay lift up one side and start forming a roll. Push the clay down with a rolling movement using the palms of your hands, folding it over and over again. Continue pushing and folding the clay until you have formed a fairly smooth roll. Then start to knead the roll in a circular fashion. Push your weight onto the clay at the top and twist it down, pushing round. Again, use the palms of your hands. If you are right handed use your right hand to do the pushing, and let your left hand pull the clay round — vice versa if you are left handed.

6 Keep repeating this special sequence. This really pushes all the air bubbles out. If you find the technique difficult to do at first don't worry — it is a skill you will acquire with practice. You may prefer just to keep pushing and folding the clay over into a smooth roll for the time being. Remember to keep a scraper near at hand to clean off the surface of the table from time to time. If you can wedge and knead on a marble surface, so much the better. The whole process of kneading clay is similar to kneading dough except that the object is to produce a pliable, even clay without air bubbles.

5

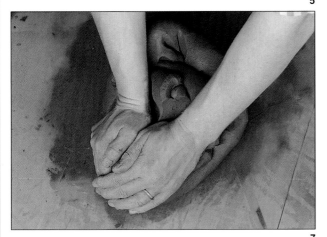

6

7

8

7 Check that the table is clean for the final stage. Then pat the roll into a 'horizontal' log shape to burst any remaining air bubbles. Pat it quite hard as you square up the edges. Then turn it upright and square the ends on the table. The clay is now ready for use.

8 The clay can be sliced up with cheesewire, each slice being weighed if appropriate. Any air bubbles can be seen as tiny holes and can be worked out of the clay later as you pat the slices into balls. The prepared clay can be kept in a damp box or wrapped in a damp towel.

MAKING SLIP

Slip is a ball clay mixed with water into a smooth, creamy liquid. Where slip really comes into its own is in decoration, either over large areas of a pot or applied with a slip trailer.

White slip is used to provide a background for much of the painted decoration on the pots in this book. Coloured slips are produced by adding powdered colours or stains to the basic mixture of powdered clay and water, and oxides may also be added, giving rich results.

When you are mixing slip it is important to mix up enough so that you can cover the whole pot when dipping it into the slip bin. The mixture should be the consistency of double cream, and it needs to be well sieved by hand to remove any lumps. Make sure that your coloured slips are kept in individual jars and well labelled so there is no danger of muddling them up.

1 You should wear a mask while mixing slip to avoid breathing in the fine particles of powdered clay. Mix up enough slip to fill a bin so that you can cover your pot adequately. Here, the potter is pouring 5 kg of white powdered ball clay into the bin to make a white slip.

2 Pour in water before mixing by hand. With experience you will soon be able to judge the correct amount.

3 Mix the powdered clay and water together, stirring it well with your hand, adding more water as needed. You are aiming for a smooth liquid the consistency of double cream. Smooth out lumps with your hands as much as possible. Mechanical mixers are available, but you would need a fairly large mixer for this amount of slip. It is, of course, cheaper and more fun to mix by hand.

4 Keep mixing the powdered clay and water together with your hand until it is fairly smooth and there are just a few lumps left. To ensure smoothness all the liquid must now be sieved. The whole process of mixing slip is quite a long job, so do allow plenty of time.

5 Ladle the mixed slip through an 80 mesh sieve into a large slip bin.

6 Help the slip through the sieve by pushing it with a sieve brush. Keep your mask on as a safety precaution all through the process of mixing slip.

7 You can also push the slip through the sieve with the palm of your hand flat against the mesh, moving it back and forth.

8

9

10

8 Then ladle the whole bin of slip through a 120 mesh sieve into another slip bin. Use smooth-sided bins if possible, they are much easier to keep clean. Use the same action with the flat of your hand or a sieve brush to make sure that the slip is completely free of lumps.

9 If at the end of this process the slip still feels a little lumpy then sieve it again through a 120 mesh sieve. You may find it easier to push the last drops through the sieve with a rubber kidney.

10 To make a coloured glaze you will need mixed white slip, powdered underglaze colours, a small 120 mesh sieve, a spoon for measuring and a container to keep the coloured slip in.

11 Place a small 120 mesh sieve on top of a container and measure in the amount of powdered colour you want. For a small pot of coloured slip you will need about three-quarters of a level teaspoonful, but again experience will help you. It may be as well to measure out the amounts accurately at first.

11

12

13

12 Pour a small amount of slip into the sieve and stir. Use a ladle to pour so that you can do this steadily and control the amount of slip.

13 Stir the slip until the colour is even, then push it through the sieve into the container. Label it so that the coloured slip is clearly marked.

14

COLOURED SLIPS

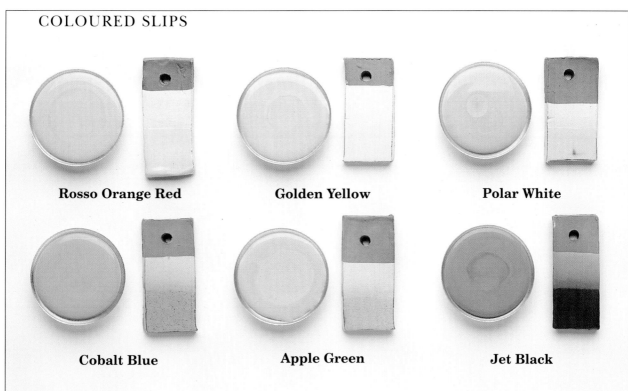

Rosso Orange Red

Golden Yellow

Polar White

Cobalt Blue

Apple Green

Jet Black

APPLYING SLIP

The technique of applying slip is fairly simple, and it will not take you long to master the knack. The trick is to give the pots a slight twist or shake of the hand when they are brought out of the slip so that any drips are avoided.

Usually the inside of a pot is slipped first to avoid smudging the outside. The slip is ladled into the pot, then poured back into the slip bin, making sure that the rim is covered. The pot should be evenly covered, and any slip that gets on to parts that should remain unslipped can be wiped off with a damp sponge. Any drips that do occur can be rubbed down with sandpaper when the slip is dry. Small pots can be dipped directly into the slip. Try to keep a sharp division between the slipped and unslipped areas of your pot to define the decoration.

1 Support a large bowl in one hand and pour the slip in from a ladle. You can see how important the consistency of the slip is — it should be like double cream. If it is too thin it will not cover the pot properly, and if too thick will tend to form unsightly lumps and drips. The method shown here is suitable for slipping as a background to painted decoration, but if you are applying slip as decoration itself you can use a brush.

2 Swill the slip around inside the bowl. Pour it back into the slip bin, twisting the pot in your hands so that the slip covers the rim. You may need to repeat the process to make sure that the edges are covered. Give the pot a little shake so that the slip does not collect at the bottom.

3 With a large bowl such as this the potter is not slipping the outside. Wipe around the edge of the rim with a damp sponge to make a clean line, and remove any odd dabs of slip on the sides of the pot in the same way.

2

1

3

4 With a small pot such as this bowl it is quite likely that you will also wish to slip the outside. Slip the inside first in the usual way, then dip the pot upside down into the slip, holding it by the foot. Make sure the pot is leather-hard before dipping the outside.

5 Plunge the pot right into the slip, up to the foot. Try to hold the pot straight so that an even line forms around the foot, leaving a clear demarcation between the slipped and unslipped areas. You may need to exert quite a lot of pressure with your hands to support the pot.

4

5

6 As you lift the pot from the slip transfer it to one hand and give it a smooth twist round in your hand to loosen any drips. If you are slipping a more complicated shape, such as a jug or cup with a handle, start the twist by the handle so that if any drips do form they will tend to be on the sides. They can then be rubbed down with sandpaper when the slip is dry.

6

FIRING AND PACKING A KILN

In order to harden the clay so that a pot may be put to practical use, and to preserve it, it must be fired in a kiln. Kilns may be powered or fired by electricity, gas, wood, oil or solid fuel — and the type you choose depends mainly on the ware or clay you are firing.

If you are working in earthenware then you are likely to find an electric kiln most suitable. Should you wish to fire stoneware, however, you may need to reduce the temperature quickly and you will find that a gas-fired kiln gives you more control. Raku clay can be fired in a conventional or home-made kiln.

Other factors to bear in mind are the cost of running your kiln and its location. The amount of space you have available will dictate its size, as will the number and size of pots you wish to fire. Both front-loading and top-loading kilns are available. Whichever you choose, make sure that there is adequate ventilation in your studio to carry away harmful fumes. Another feature to look for is a safety lock on the door which immediately cuts off the power when the kiln is opened.

The crucial point about firing a kiln is the control and accurate measurement of temperature. A pyrometer or temperature gauge on the outside of the kiln lets you know the exact temperature the kiln has reached inside. Since different clays fire at different temperatures potters also use pyrometric ceramic cones inside the kiln. These graded cones melt at certain temperatures, thus indicating when the pot has been fired at the correct temperature.

The results of your firings will all be slightly different. Keep a log comparing the times and temperatures so that you will be able to work out future firings more accurately.

Biscuit firing
A pot is usually biscuit fired prior to being glazed if it is to be further decorated with colour. This first firing takes place when the pot has dried out. You

A selection of front-loading and top-loading electric kilns suitable for domestic use and for the potter with limited space. Heated by elements, the kilns are insulated with fire brick, backed by ceramic fibre. They are fitted with a variety of modifications for temperature control. Safety devices include a switch that automatically cuts the electrical supply when the door is opened. The pots are stacked on shelves, and the progress of the firing can be monitored through a spyhole in the side.

can tell that the clay is ready by its lighter colour and by feel. Pots are fired slowly to the temperature required for the ware. Since they will not stick together in biscuit firing, pots can be stacked tightly in the kiln. It does not matter if they touch, and one pot can be stacked inside another as long as they are well supported.

Glaze firing

Glaze firing is the final firing after glaze has been applied to give a glassy, protective finish to the pot. Pots are fired rapidly at first, but the process is slowed down when the glaze starts to melt. No pot must touch another when packed into the kiln or they will stick. The colour of the kiln inside changes from black to red through bright orange to pale yellow as it gets hotter. You can check on this and the cones through the spyhole in the side, and you will see the pot glistening when it is ready.

Kiln furniture

1 Bat or shelf used for stacking. These should be protected from glaze by a coating of batwash — a mixture of china clay, alumina and water.
2 Tubular props support the shelves.
3 Castellated props interlock for different heights.
4 Interlocking extending props extend the height of tubular props. They can also be used on their own.
5 Stilts support pots clear of the kiln shelf.
6 Pyrometric ceramic cones are designed to melt when a certain temperature is reached in the kiln.

Chapter 4
Effects and finishes

For many the most exciting part of ceramics is letting the imagination run riot in the choice of decoration. You may decide to keep the pot in its original clay colour and add interest in the form of texture or to incise or stamp a design in the clay. Keep an eye open for suitable objects and materials to use — a simple item employed in an unusual way can make a pot look stunning.

If you want to colour your pot, however, there is a wide range of finishes — among them, paints and glazes. The approach to painting pottery differs slightly from painting on canvas as the colours change in the firing processes, and you must become familiar with them to achieve the result you desire. But the inspiration and ideas come in exactly the same way — from watching what is around you, observing nature and learning from other artists' and potters' work.

It is in the area of glazes that pottery allows the greatest experimentation. This is a vast subject and many potters spend years perfecting their own recipes. There are many glazes available commercially but you will find it far more fun to try mixing your own.

Effects and finishes

TEXTURES AND SPRIGGING TOOLS

One of the easiest ways of decorating your ceramics is simply to impress a pattern on the clay. There are so many readily available objects that you can use to produce either an overall effect or more precise 'punctuation' of the pot. Try to fit the decoration to the form so that whatever you apply complements the pot and becomes an integral part of it.

Choose objects that will leave a sharp impression and will come away from the clay cleanly — any foreign body in the clay may cause the pot to explode or crack in the firing process.

You can make your own stamps or 'sprigging' tools by rolling a coil of clay and impressing a pattern on the top that can be reproduced on your pots over and over again.

Sponge and foam stoppers from tablet bottles can also be shaped and cut to make interesting and unusual printing pads which can be dipped in coloured slips or paint. Painting the slip on unevenly can produce some interesting effects, as can dipping the pad into two or three colours and merging them together. This technique can be used to produce stamps with an abstract design or very precise outlines.

Build up a collection of possible stamps for use on your pots and keep them together in a box. Anything that can give a clean and interesting impression is worth keeping. The patterns made by natural objects such as sea shells, nuts and wood seem to complement clay very well, and more everyday objects such as screws, keys and bottle tops often produce surprising effects when part of a repeat pattern. Small scraps of open-weave material can be used as an overall texture on large areas. Try the stamps out on a spare slab of clay.

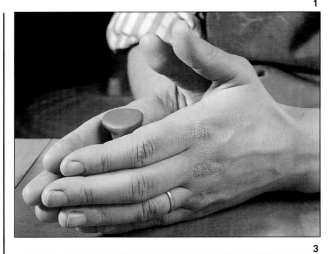

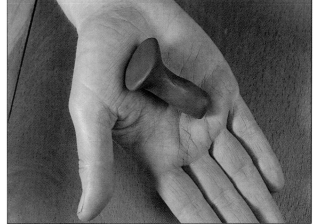

1 A permanent clay stamp or sprigging tool can easily be made by rolling a coil of clay upright in your hands. In this case the top has been slightly flattened with the fingertips, but it can be of whatever shape, and size, you choose. You could make a completely flat sprigging tool without a 'handle', depending on the pattern you are aiming for.

2 The coil has been formed into a small mushroom shape so that it is easy to hold. Skewer a hole through the coil at the end of the handle so that it can be hung up on a piece of string. You could make a whole series of sprigging tools for different effects.

3 Mark a pattern on the top of the mushroom. Here the potter is using a wooden modelling tool. Remember that an impressed pattern will give an embossed effect when the stamp is used on clay, and vice versa. Wait for the clay to harden, then fire the sprigging tool.

4 The sprigging tool can be pressed straight on to the pot, or it can be used to make medallions as here. Place a small knob of clay on the pot, then press the sprigging tool on, removing it carefully.

PAINTS

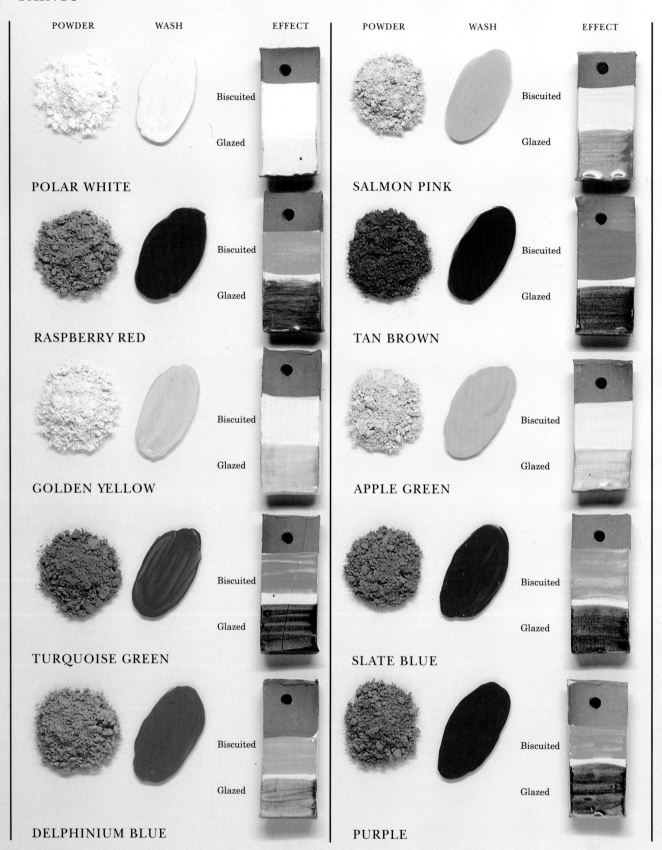

POWDER	WASH	EFFECT		POWDER	WASH	EFFECT

POLAR WHITE — Biscuited / Glazed

RASPBERRY RED — Biscuited / Glazed

GOLDEN YELLOW — Biscuited / Glazed

TURQUOISE GREEN — Biscuited / Glazed

DELPHINIUM BLUE — Biscuited / Glazed

SALMON PINK — Biscuited / Glazed

TAN BROWN — Biscuited / Glazed

APPLE GREEN — Biscuited / Glazed

SLATE BLUE — Biscuited / Glazed

PURPLE — Biscuited / Glazed

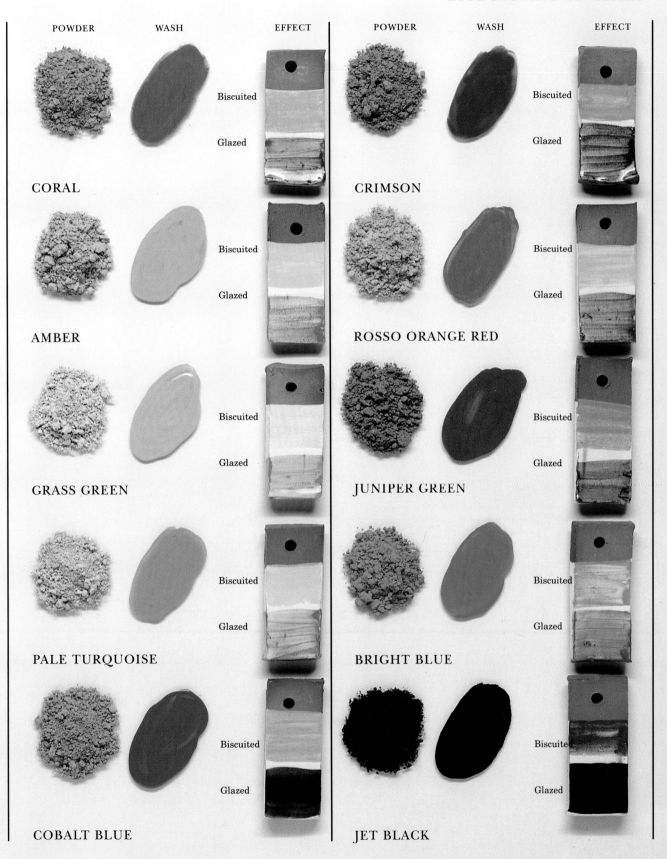

POWDER	WASH	EFFECT		POWDER	WASH	EFFECT
		Biscuited				Biscuited
		Glazed				Glazed
CORAL				**CRIMSON**		
		Biscuited				Biscuited
		Glazed				Glazed
AMBER				**ROSSO ORANGE RED**		
		Biscuited				Biscuited
		Glazed				Glazed
GRASS GREEN				**JUNIPER GREEN**		
		Biscuited				Biscuited
		Glazed				Glazed
PALE TURQUOISE				**BRIGHT BLUE**		
		Biscuited				Biscuited
		Glazed				Glazed
COBALT BLUE				**JET BLACK**		

GLAZES

Although we tend to think of glazes as the glassy finish on pots, glazes can be matt as well as shiny. Their main function, however, is to provide a protective coating on the pot, and particularly to make it waterproof.

There are many commercial ready-made glazes available, but it is more fun to make your own. Many books are available with countless recipes you can use. You can also make up your own recipes as long as you include the three main constituents: silica, which is a glass former, a flux (such as feldspar, calcium, barium or potash, or a combination of these) to help it melt, and alumina to make it adhere to the pot.

The glaze you use must be suitable for and 'fit' the ware. This is important decoratively — for instance, one would tend to decorate a fine porcelain with an attractive glaze which fuses with the clay and enhances its translucency — and it is essential technically. The glaze and clay must shrink at the same rate in the firing process or unwanted crazing will occur.

Glaze Recipes

Clear glaze for earthenware

Lead bisilicate	68%
China clay	12%
Cornish stone	15%
Whiting	5%

Clear glaze for stoneware or porcelain

Potash feldspar	35%
Dolomite	10%
Whiting	10%
China clay	17%
Quartz	28%

1 Mixing a glaze involves accurate measuring of proportions and fine sieving to produce a liquid that is the consistency of single cream. The ingredients are each weighed out as a percentage of the whole glaze mixture, and you should wear a mask throughout the process to avoid breathing in the fine glaze dust. Glaze is prepared and applied to pots in a similar way to slip, and it can be stored in labelled containers ready for future use. Any dabs of glaze which get on to areas where it is not wanted must be wiped off immediately with a damp sponge so that the glaze does not stick in the kiln.

2 After weighing out all the ingredients into a bucket pour in water. Mix the glaze by hand, breaking the powdery lumps in the mixture between your fingers. Introduce more water gradually as necessary. You are aiming for the consistency of single cream.

3 The glaze mixture is sieved through a 60 mesh sieve, then a 100 mesh sieve, and finally a 120 mesh sieve to produce a smooth liquid. Push it through with the flat of your hand working back and forth, or use a rubber kidney.

It is the addition of oxides that give colour to a glaze, and their proportions and method of firing both have their effect on the final result. Many potters develop their own glaze recipes which give their pots a distinctive style. It is useful to try out your colours on a set of test tiles, using a variety of glazes on a particular clay and firing them at different temperatures. Every firing is different and even established potters cannot reproduce the exact effect every time.

Raku test dishes

Three glazes were used on these dishes. The left-hand row were glazed with a clear glaze, the centre row with an opaque white crackle glaze and the right-hand row with a turquoise green glaze.

The left half of all of these dishes was glazed, and then stripes of copper carbonate, red iron oxide, cobalt oxide and manganese dioxide were painted right across the dishes before the right half of each dish was glazed. Thus each dish shows the effect of overglaze and underglaze colouring.

The nine dishes were all fired in a raku kiln. Reading across, the **top row** were simply taken from the kiln and allowed to cool till they could be handled. The **second row** were taken from the kiln, then placed on a bed of sawdust and covered with a dustbin lid for about five minutes before being quenched in water and cleaned with wire wool. The **third row** were taken from the kiln, then buried in sawdust for about twenty minutes, quenched and cleaned with wire wool. In this last example the reduction firing (see p. 134) has taken oxygen from the oxides turning them into base metal and producing a metallic lustre on the dishes.

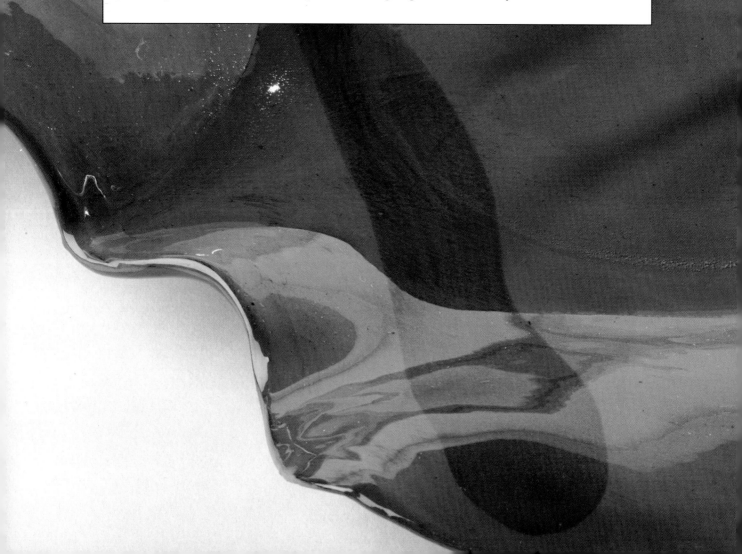

Chapter 5
Building by hand

You have been introduced to clay, the various techniques essential in working it, and had a glimpse of some of the means available for decorating ceramics. So now let us start actually making a pot.

Building by hand is a method that has been employed by potters for thousands of years. For many it is an enjoyable way to use clay and to create interesting shapes. It offers a great deal of flexibility often denied to those with no great experience of using a wheel, and allows you to develop your imagination and style. Many professional potters specialize in hand-building.

There are two basic ways of building by hand — using slabs and using coils. This chapter suggests projects for both of these methods, and introduces important techniques for joining. If the joints of a pot are weak they are likely to pull apart, leaving you with a pot of little real use and a sense of disappointment.

The projects also show how simple decoration can complement the form of a pot. Some of the most exciting decoration is built up as a pot progresses. Equally, it is not always necessary to decide what you are going to make before you start.

Basic techniques

USING A MOULD

One of the easiest ways to make a pot is to roll a basic slab of clay and shape it by draping it over a mould such as a bowl or basin. An enormous variety of shapes can be produced from moulds and, even if you have never worked with clay before, this method will soon boost your confidence and encourage you to try out different ideas.

More or less any object can be used as a mould, providing it is clean and does not contain anything that will adhere to the clay. Bowls, basins, pieces of wood, large stones and bottles will all give interesting shapes.

You may find a large clay slab a bit cumbersome to handle at first, so make sure that the mould you choose to start with is a fairly simple shape and of reasonable size. Remember that it is not necessary to reproduce the exact shape of the mould. In fact, the more your pot differs from the original the more individual it will look. Use the mould as a guide which you can adapt as much as you wish to give you creative scope. The less slavishly you try to shape the clay around the mould the more opportunity you have to introduce your own style.

Moulded pots are a useful way of making an item quickly, and often an unusual shape will inspire you to experiment with new decorative techniques.

1 Before starting to roll out the slab of clay place some sheeting or hessian on the table. This stops the clay sticking to a wooden surface and also gives an interesting texture to the clay. Use a long rolling pin that will protrude over the edge of the slab — a wooden towel rail is ideal. Roll evenly in all directions, working your hands from the centre to the edges and back. To ensure that you roll out the clay to an even thickness it is useful to place two matching pieces of wood at either side of the slab so that you roll down to the depth of the wood. Try to keep the material reasonably flat or it will impress creases on the clay causing weaknesses in those areas when it is later fired.

2 When the slab has been rolled evenly on one side, lift it carefully and turn it over, again placing it on the sheeting. Stretch the sheeting slightly to check that there are no creases, and briefly roll the other side of the slab. Then place your mould, in this case a bowl, upside down on the table. Make sure that the surface of the mould is clean and free from dust or particles that might stick to the clay. Lift the slab with a piece of cloth, supporting them both between your hands and gently drape them over the mould. It is not necessary to be precise about positioning the slab centrally over the bowl — slightly off-centre may give a more interesting shape and the chance to enhance it with a particular decorative feature.

3 Peel the cloth carefully up and away from the slab of clay. As you do so, the rounded edges of the slab will probably flop down, falling into a natural shape over the mould. Guide the edges with your fingertips while you remove the cloth, emphasizing the natural folds to create a pleasing effect. Then press the slab of clay gently on to the bottom of the mould to fix the clay firmly into the desired shape.

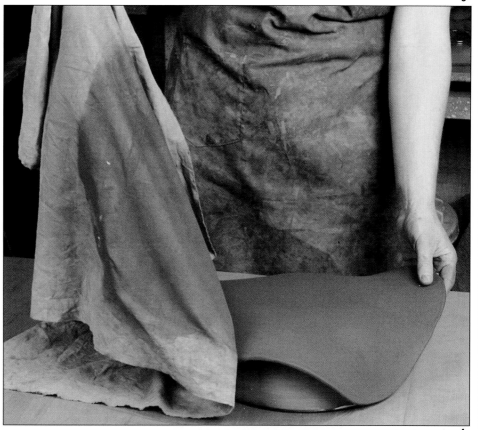

4 Press the folds firmly down with your hands, but be careful not to exert too much pressure or you may crack the clay. A final light roll over the base of the mould helps to define the inner impression of the mould on the clay and to ensure a smooth base on your pot. Then leave the clay to dry and harden. You can slide the mould with the slab across the table to transfer it to another surface if necessary.

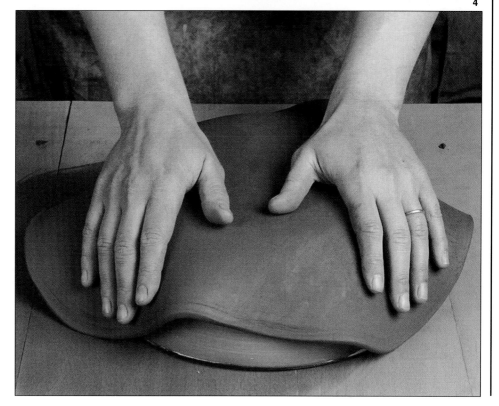

Serving platter

BUILDING BY HAND

Producing an attractive and functional pot fairly quickly is always encouraging to a beginner, and many experienced potters may also occasionally enjoy a break from using the wheel. Making a slab dish is an excellent way of getting a feel for clay — understanding its plasticity and its 'breaking' point. It is important to remember that the slab must be rolled evenly to the right thickness so that no areas of weakness can occur in the finished pot.

The technique of using a mould is used to make the serving platter shown in this project. By allowing the edges of the slab to 'fall' into natural folds the result is a free-flowing form that gives enormous scope for decoration. The size of the slab also suggested the function of the finished dish — ideal for a serving platter.

Feet were added for the practical purpose of lifting the platter when placed on a table, and also for aesthetic reasons. With the platter raised slightly it appears to be 'floating', allowing the full effect of its folds and undulations to be seen from the side. There are numerous ways in which feet can be attached. You may prefer to add loops of clay, for instance, but you will find that three feet are much more stable than four on a dish like this.

The wavy edges of the platter soon suggested possible ideas for decoration to the potter and she decided on a summer sailing theme. Sea green slip was painted on with a broad brush for the background and waves were then painted in using white slip. Tiny racing yachts were outlined with a thin brush, then filled in with colour to complete the scene.

1

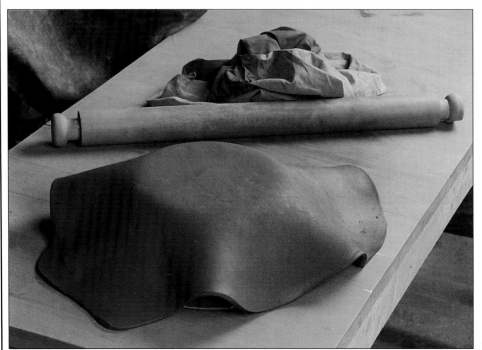

Materials
Rolling pin
Cloth
Potter's knife
Pieces of wood
Paintbrushes

Colours
Turquoise Green
Slate Blue
Juniper Green
Coral
Polar White
Purple
Golden Yellow

1 An attractive serving platter can be made simply by draping a rolled slab over a mould such as a bowl. After positioning the slab of clay on the mould press it down firmly and guide the folds into a pleasing shape with your hands. Then roll quickly across the base using short movements, exerting just enough pressure to impress the mould on the slab, but not too much to cut into the clay. The base needs to be even so that the platter will stand firmly. Leave the pot to harden and dry before adding the feet.

2 Before attaching the feet place three small balls of clay on the base to indicate their positions. Then, with a potter's knife, score on the base of the platter where the first is to go.

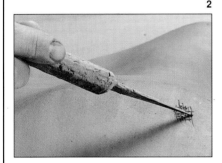

3 Put slip on the scoring of the base of the platter and then attach the first ball of clay to make a foot, pushing it down firmly. The other two feet are attached similarly, first scoring, then adding a little slip before pushing down the ball of clay. Make sure that the feet are placed equidistant from each other so that they balance. Three feet are put on because they give more stability than four.

4 The feet can be left as balls of clay and slightly flattened, or incised with a pattern or modelled as the potter has chosen to do here. By pushing down on each side of the ball of clay with a piece of wood you can make a four-sided foot with a flattened edge. The extra pressure exerted also helps the foot to adhere more strongly.

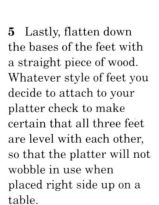

5 Lastly, flatten down the bases of the feet with a straight piece of wood. Whatever style of feet you decide to attach to your platter check to make certain that all three feet are level with each other, so that the platter will not wobble in use when placed right side up on a table.

6 The wavy edges of the platter suggested a sea scene decoration and so the dish is covered in a background colour of sea green — white slip with a little green and blue mixed in. It is applied with a broad brush, starting with the centre of the dish and working up and around. Be careful not to apply slip too thickly or it will crack in drying. You may even prefer to leave some areas very thinly covered so that glimpses of the clay colour can be seen underneath.

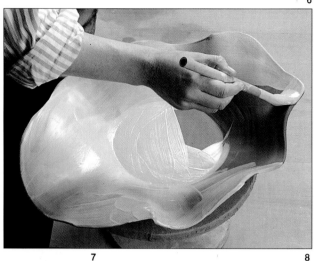

8 After the slip has dried — usually very quickly — the platter is biscuit fired. The tiny yachts are then painted in with bright colours to contrast with the subdued background of the sea. Action in the scene is introduced by depicting them ploughing through the waves, and as a final touch racing numbers are painted in. Don't worry too much if you make mistakes at this stage. They can be wiped off with a damp sponge, allowing you to start again.

7 When the background slip has dried, brush on the waves. Dip a broad brush into both white and green slips and make free-flowing strokes. The tip of the brush is turned slightly as it is swept across so that the width of the stroke varies, giving an impression of the movement of waves. With a decorative theme such as this the quicker such strokes can be painted the better the final effect.

9

9 With the serving platter now biscuit-fired and the painting complete, the dish is now ready for glazing. This will fix and protect the decoration with a glassy finish.

10 The pot is covered by ladling glaze into the centre and swishing it around, pouring the excess back into the bucket over the edges.

Twist the platter carefully in your hand to make sure that the top is covered with glaze, then wipe off any drips underneath with a damp sponge.

10

11

11 After firing the glazed platter emerges from the kiln as an attractive, functional and individual dish.

TIPS AND HINTS

To make sure the edges of the pot are smooth rub gently with a cloth while the clay is soft.

Basic techniques

COILING

Coiling is a basic method that has been used to make pots for thousands of years. The pinching technique of joining the coils together allows you a great deal of control over the form of your pot as you can plan its shape as each coil is added.

Roll even coils of a reasonable length and join them every three coils or so, making certain that each layer is firmly smoothed in to the next.

1 There are two ways to make a base for a coiled pot. The quickest method is simply to flatten out a ball of clay between the palms of your hands — something which you will be able to do quite easily with experience. Another way is to roll out a slab of clay and then use a potter's knife to cut out a piece of clay to the shape and size you require, peeling away the outer clay. Here the potter is using a banding wheel on which to cut out a circular piece of clay.

2 You can use the left-over clay from the slab to make your first coil. The quickest way to roll coils is horizontally in your hands, but this takes some practice, so it is easier to start by rolling coils vertically on a table. Roll the clay smoothly and gently, working it with even pressure from your fingertips to your palms and moving your hands from the centre of the coil to the outsides so that the coil gradually lengthens.

1

2

3

3 Place the end of the first coil on the base of the pot, pushing it down with your index finger. Then gradually guide the whole coil into position, continuing to push down with your index finger and keeping the coil in a circular shape with your thumb and fingers. Your other hand meanwhile supports the rest of the coil that has still to be joined. Don't be in too much of a hurry with this process. It is important that the first coil is fixed firmly in the correct position.

4

5

6

4 To make sure that the first coil is firmly fixed to the base of the pot smooth the edge of the coil down onto the base with the top of your index finger, working gradually around the inside of the pot.

5 Add two or three more coils, making sure that they are all rolled evenly, then push them firmly down on to the layer below. Use the same movement with your hands so that you are actually using a pinching technique, smoothing the coils between your fingers and thumb. Try to keep the top of the pot level and check on the evenness of your coils by rotating the banding wheel. You can cut off any stray bits of clay with a potter's knife. Also check the shape of your pot as you build it up, again by turning the banding wheel.

6 After three layers or so join the outsides of the coils, smoothing the clay with your fingertips in a downwards movement. Add more coils, smoothing inside and out as you progress. Coiling allows you to be completely in control of the shape you are building, but you must remember to keep that control. Turn the banding wheel every so often to check that the profile of the pot is as you wish. If you want the pot to curve out then set the coils slightly on the edge. Keep turning the banding wheel and smooth the pot into shape with your fingers and a metal kidney. Use a potter's knife to tidy it up inside and out if necessary.

Flower vase

BUILDING BY HAND

The flower vase in this project owes much to the traditional ware shapes of Japanese and Chinese coil pots. These distinctive pots, produced as functional items, seemed to combine stability with elegance, a combination that is not always easy to achieve when throwing a pot at speed.

As the potter is in total control of every stage in building a coil pot it is possible to produce shapes with this method which are extremely difficult on the wheel unless you are very experienced. This flower vase was built up by careful positioning of the size of the coils to give a bellied shape, before adding a straight neck which opens out into a wide mouth.

The potter has emphasized each change of direction in the pot with clay outlines, and given a different surface texture to each section to add interest and variety. Finally, she rounded the base to give a less solid impression.

Materials
Banding wheel
Potter's knife
Metal kidney
Plastic credit card
Throwing hook
Water spray
Wooden modelling tools
Textured cloth

1 Continue building up the coils of your pot, increasing its size by placing them slightly on the edge, and joining them with a pinching technique. When you have built up to a certain height make sure that the inside of the pot is finished by smoothing it with a metal kidney. It is important to do this before the pot gets too high or you will not be able to reach inside.

2 Smooth the outside of the pot with a metal kidney. (A plastic credit card is also useful here.) Keep turning the banding wheel to check the profile of the pot, so that you are in control of the shape throughout the whole process. It is often helpful to make a sketch of the shape you want to produce beforehand and then refer back to it frequently.

3 Start moving the shape of the pot inwards by placing the coils slightly in on the edge. Continue adding coils, always one layer at a time, shaping and smoothing inside and out with a metal kidney as you go. Check that the top of the pot is level and if necessary carefully even it off with a potter's knife.

4 The last coil goes on for the belly of the vase. Pat inside with a wooden throwing hook to help round out the shape. Then tap the pot gently around the top with the back of a wooden spoon — this gives a slight angle so that light falling on it will define the shape. Check against your sketch and use a potter's knife to remove any excess clay at the top. If you wish to add a decorative ledge to your pot then incise a guideline for a coil. Here the potter has marked a line about halfway down the pot.

5 Pinch the base of the coil forming the ledge so that it adheres firmly. The bottom of the ledge is then smoothed down with the fingertips and the top smoothed up, following up with a metal kidney. Finish off by turning the banding wheel and shaping the outline of the ledge with a wet chamois. It is a matter of personal choice whether you add a ledge and exactly where you place it. You must judge for yourself according to the proportions of your pot. Here the ledge is important for the final look of the flower vase — it gives the pot something to 'spring' from.

6 The top of the vase is to widen out into a mouth, so to provide a neck for this build two or three coils straight up, pinching and smoothing as you go. Again, pay attention to the inside as it will be difficult to reach later. Add a coiled ledge at the bottom of the neck in the same way as earlier, incising a guideline first.

55

7

8

9

7 When the upper ledge has been added and smoothed you can start building out from the top of the neck. First add a coil just inside, pushing down with your fingers to make a mitre so that the fluted part will have a base to sit on. As you add increasing sizes of coil, building outwards, pinch and smooth them with your fingers as you go. The clay will be fairly fragile here so take great care. Smooth around the inside with a metal kidney, supporting the outside with the palm of your hand. Press in the neck of the vase slightly by smoothing and pulling down gently with your finger. Then smooth the outside of the fluted neck with a metal kidney. Finally, add a coil on top to make the rim of the vase.

8 Pinch and smooth the top coil of the vase to make a rim. Then finish off again with a metal kidney, supporting the inside of the pot with your other hand, and turning the banding wheel to check the shape.

9 The final shaping of the rim is done by pressing it between your thumb and first finger, gradually working your way all round the pot. Again, use a metal kidney, scraping up from the bottom of the neck to smooth and define the outside shape until you are satisfied with it.

10

10 Now to try out some decorative techniques. The outer edge of the rim of the vase is decorated by incising it with the end of a wooden modelling tool. Rotate your hand slightly while you do this to make sure you achieve clean, defined edges. Support the top of the pot with the thumb and fingers of your other hand.

11

11 Make the fluting on the top part of the belly of the vase by simply pulling down with a thin wooden spatula. Then tidy the flutes by pulling up the spatula from the bottom, giving them clean edges. You could use a number of different tools for the flutes — the end of a spoon, for instance, or a cheesewire for broader bands. You may prefer to apply completely different decoration.

12

12 The bottom of the vase is textured by pressing on and gently peeling away a square of rough cloth. Again, you may prefer a different technique, but this simple method is very effective.

13 Give the vase an extra finish by sharpening the shapes of the surfaces with a metal kidney. Hold the pot on its side to give more control, and to avoid too many clay particles falling inside.

14 Finally the base of the vase is rounded off slightly by rolling it around the table surface. You can also help to round it off in your hands or even place the bowl of a ladle inside the pot to help shape it. The vase is now ready for firing.

13

14

Basic techniques

MITRING CORNERS

If a slab dish with joined sides is to serve as a useful container it is important that its joints are strong. Its design needs to be planned thoroughly beforehand so that you can be sure the pieces will fit together well. You can minimize the risk of the sides not matching properly and the problem of weak joints by cutting the slabs using a template and mitring the corners.

Remember to allow enough depth for turning the sides up when working out your design, and make sure that the corners are at right angles. You will find that measuring and drawing your plan on graph paper is the easiest way to produce an accurate template.

Mitred corners provide maximum support and can also be embellished so that the corners of the dish become a decorative feature.

Materials
Cloth
Pieces of wood
Paper or card
Rolling pin
Scissors
Potter's knife
Board

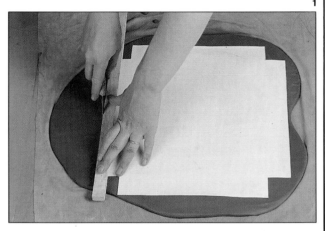

1 Make sure that your rolling pin is clean by wiping it with a damp sponge, and then roll out a slab of clay. Place your template made out of paper or card on the slab. It is particularly important that you have measured the sides accurately and that the corners are square. Cut out around the template with a potter's knife, slicing the top surfaces of the corners at an angle of forty-five degrees so that they can join together in a mitred corner. Then peel away the template.

2 Transfer the slab to a board. Place a wooden rule or straight piece of wood along the inner edge of the slab so that it aligns with the corners. This will help to support the sides when they are joined so that they are straight and firm.

3 Fold up the edge of the dish towards you, flattening and supporting it as you do so with another piece of wood. Join the edges together when the second side has been folded up, and so on for the others.

4 The strength and usefulness of the dish will depend on strong joints, so after you have joined all four corners go round again, pushing the edges together to make sure they are really firm. Smooth them off with your fingertips. If you wish, you can add an extra coil of clay in the corners to help disguise any inaccuracy in the cutting of the slab, especially if the edges do not match exactly.

5 Make the coil long enough to overlap the top of the dish slightly. Squeeze it into the corner with a piece of wood so that it adheres firmly. As well as reinforcing the corner these additions make the pot look visually stronger and interesting.

4

5

6

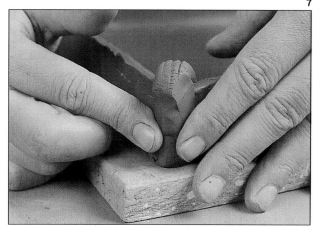

7

6 The corner coils can be decorated to make an attractive feature. Here lines have been impressed with a modelling tool against the coil after it was squeezed into place. Finally, bend the top of the coil over and push it well in to secure it on the outside edge of the dish.

7 Smooth the top of the coil into the sides of the dish with your fingertips. When all the corners have been clamped together place a cloth over the top edge of the sides and rub over it with a piece of wood or bowl of a spoon. This removes any rough edges that would harden up during firing and might cut you when handling the dish.

Hors d'oeuvres dish

BUILDING BY HAND

This hors d'oeuvres dish provides an ideal surface for a number of decorative techniques. As clay is such a pliable material it is easy to impress pattern on it, and although the potter here used old textile printing blocks, any number of readily available household items can be used to produce attractive effects. You can also make your own stamps and sprigging tools. Further ways of decorating with coloured slip are shown in this project — a 'paper-resist' technique in which slip is applied with a pressurized air spray over paper which is later removed, and slip 'trailing'.

Materials
Pieces of wood
Cloth stamps
Sprigging tools
Coloured slip
Pressurized air spray
Newspaper
Slip trailer

Colours
Turquoise Green
Slate Blue
Juniper Green
Jet Black

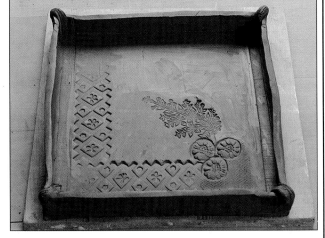

1 The slab dish is ready to be decorated. Here the potter is impressing a pattern using old textile printing blocks, being careful to apply an even pressure.

2 Now the potter is producing a pattern from a sprigging tool she has made from clay. Peel away the stamp carefully after you have applied it, to give clean edges to the pattern. Try to work out the design to some extent before you use a stamp. If you do want to change the decoration, however, you can smooth the slab out again with a credit card or a metal kidney.

3 The dish showing the finished impressed design is now ready to be slipped. Pour the slip in with a ladle, and move the dish around in your hands to make sure the slip flows into all the corners. Then pour the excess back into the slip bucket. Paint slip onto the rims and over the tops of the decorative corners with a broad brush. Wipe away drips from the outside of the dish with a damp sponge.

4

5

6

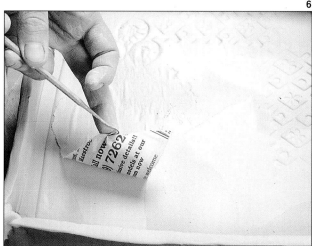

7

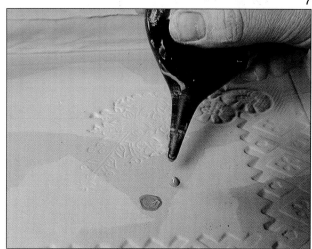

4 You can use a paper-resist technique to add another layer of slip. Simply tear up pieces of newspaper and place them on the dish to make a pleasing abstract design, or cut out specific shapes for a precisely planned pattern or image. Smooth down the paper with your fingertips to help it adhere.

5 Now spray coloured slip onto the slab dish, making sure that it covers the dish well, including the pieces of paper. The spray is applied with a pressurized air canister, the attachment tube feeding from a container of slip, and it is advisable to wear a face mask for this process. You will find it easier to spray evenly if the dish revolves on a banding wheel. If the paper lifts press it gently down again with your fingertips.

6 Peel back and remove the pieces of paper with a dentist's tool or crochet hook. Underneath will be revealed the first layer of slip, giving a two-colour effect to the dish. You could, of course, apply several layers of colour using this technique.

7 When the second coat of slip is dry you can add further decoration. Here the potter is adding spots of black slip using a slip trailer. Make sure that the slip is fairly liquid or it will blob, and try the trailer out before applying the slip to the dish.

8

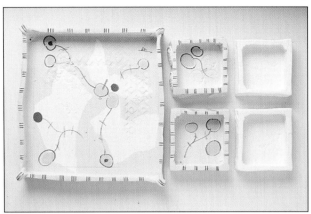

8 The dish with the three forms of decoration so far applied — stamping, paper-resist and slip trailing. Four smaller dishes were made to fit inside the slab dish, following the same technique of cutting around a template and using pieces of wood to join the sides. The coils in the corners were not made so prominent, however, as they do not need so much visual strength. The potter decided to finish off the design on the inside of the large dish by adding flowing black lines with a thin brush, and decorating the rim. The smaller dishes were decorated using the same techniques and colours but with a variety of design. Finally, all the dishes were glazed.

9 The hors d'oeuvres dish after firing. The smaller dishes were slipped and decorated around the sides by incising lines, painting or adding on clay pressed with a sprigging tool. All complement and tie in with the larger dish with its plain, unglazed sides.

Chapter 6

Using the wheel

The main attraction for many people interested in ceramics is getting to work on the potter's wheel. Learning to control the clay and guiding it to form an attractive and functional pot is fun and, once mastered, gives you a sense of great achievement. This chapter shows you the basic techniques needed — how to centre the clay on the wheel, throw it and define the shape and style of the pot.

For a pot to be successful, attention should be paid to detail. Its rim should indicate a clearly defined finish and the pot needs to 'rise' from a foot which complements the overall profile. Handles should look and feel firm and comfortable to hold. Rims must be smooth and not too thick — a cup must be of practical use.

Even if you are not a born artist painting and decorating your pot should be no problem — there is a wealth of decorative techniques to choose from and combine. Brush painting to suit your individual style and printing in the form of abstract designs can all enhance your ceramics, making each piece an individual item. The creative skills that you have in other areas are all put to use in pottery.

Basic techniques

CENTRING CLAY

It is important to 'centre' the clay on the wheel before throwing. Clay that is off-centre is difficult to control as the wheel exerts an outward force when revolving. It will also produce a pot that is uneven in shape or with walls that vary in thickness, resulting in weak areas. While checking that the clay is centred the potter squeezes the clay up into a cone and down again. This ensures that any tiny air bubbles are worked out of the clay.

The clay must be of an even consistency, well wedged and kneaded, but not too soft or it will be difficult to throw. Experience and practice will soon let you know when the clay feels right. While centring and throwing keep the clay and your hands moist. Try not to overwork the clay or make it too wet as it will lose its plasticity.

Materials
Turning tools
Throwing rib
Cheesewire
Chamois
Sponge

1 Place a moist, but not wet, ball of clay in the centre of the wheel. Do not slam it down hard — just tap it gently so that it sticks.

1

2

3

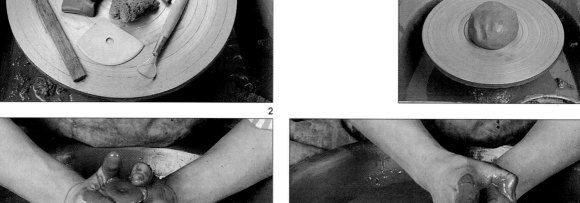

2 Turn the wheel fairly fast, squeezing the clay between the palms of your hands. By exerting pressure at the bottom of the clay gradually curve it up into a cone. This coning process works out any air bubbles from the clay. It depends entirely on the control and pressure of your hands, and you may find that you need quite a lot of practice to do it correctly. Keep your elbows in to help you exert the right amount of pressure and control.

3 Then bring the cone down again to a flattish shape. The left hand controls the clay, with not too much pressure, while the right hand pushes the cone down. The hands must work together in this action. Do not make a hollow in the centre of the clay or you will create air bubbles.

4

5

4 Gently centre the clay, moving it up into a cone and back down again, until the clay feels even and there are no air bubbles. When you are happy with this make a hollow with your fingertips to provide a base for the bowl. Then flattening the fingertips of one hand, while supported and pushing down with the other, guide the clay base into the shape you wish. Make sure that you do not push into the base so that it is too thin.

5 The pot is gradually built up into a bowl by pulling the clay from the bottom to the top of the pot and throwing the shape outwards. The work on the pot is done with both hands, but initially mainly with the inner hand. Once you are happy with the inside, however, you should work from the outside. Smooth with a small real sponge as the bowl progresses.

6

6 Here the potter is pulling up a ring from the bottom of the pot so that it rises to form a rim. A strong rim is visually important to finish off a bowl, so you need something to work on in order to shape it properly. As you guide the clay up smooth it with a sponge or a chamois.

7

7 Finish the rim off with a sponge or chamois so that it is smooth. You can alter the shape with your fingertips as you do so if necessary. While you are throwing the bowl keep an eye on its profile — the rim will need to complement the shape.

TIPS AND HINTS

If you unfortunately find an air bubble on your thrown pot, prick it with a needle.

8 Define the rim of the bowl with the edge of your nail and fingertip. A throwing rib is also useful for this job. The rim needs a strong profile to delineate the edge of the pot, so it is worth taking some care over this. Support your shaping finger with your other hand inside the pot. If the rim is angled down slightly underneath it will cast a shadow, thus emphasizing its form.

8

9

9 The bowl is now ready for adding a foot. Run a wooden turning tool around the bottom edge of the bowl. This clearly delineates where the foot of the bowl will start. Then cut the pot from the wheel with cheesewire. Sponge a little water onto the wheel. As the sides of the bowl are delicate, slide it across to remove it without damage.

ADDING A FOOT

A bowl needs a foot — for the practical purpose of having something to stand on, but also for aesthetic reasons. Just as a strong rim finishes the top so a sharply defined foot gives a bowl 'lift'.

This technique demonstrates how to add a foot to a bowl by adding a coil, then pinching and smoothing it in. Many potters, however, choose to carve or turn a foot from the base of the bowl itself, and we shall be looking at how to do this shortly.

Whichever method you choose the foot should complement the style and shape of your pot. Its depth needs to be in proportion to the bowl. A simple rule to follow in shaping the foot itself is to make sure it has three angles, so that light playing on the surfaces can delineate its edges and thus emphasize its 'spring.'

1 Centre the bowl upside down on the wheel. You can check that it is in the centre by marking a shallow line with your fingernail around the top and then observing an even line as the bowl revolves on the wheel. When the bowl is centred press three knobs of clay down firmly in a triangle formation to hold the pot in place.

2 Now with a turning tool make the shape that you require for the base of the bowl. Hold the tool against the bowl as it turns and it will gradually pare the clay away. Do not pare too much, however. Tap the clay to check its thickness. With experience you will recognize that the higher the sound the thinner the clay.

3 Mark a thin line around the base of the bowl to indicate the position of the foot. Then, with the wheel still revolving make lines around the base with a serrated turning tool where the foot is to be joined. These score lines will enable the coil of clay which will form the foot to adhere more firmly to the bowl.

4 Roll a coil of clay in your hands and as you place it on the score lines pinch it down between your finger and thumb to secure it firmly to the base of the bowl. Support the rest of the coil in your other hand.

5 This shows clearly how the coil is pinched down, leaving thumbprints around the outside edge. Once the coil is in position smooth the top over with your fingertip. This helps to form the shape of the foot and the additional slight pressure pushes the coil more firmly into the clay at the base of the bowl.

6

6 Now shape the foot with a wet chamois by smoothing the coil as the wheel revolves. Press on top with the chamois with your finger and thumb either side of the foot, squeezing gently. When you are satisfied that the foot is smooth enough, check on the angle between the bowl and the foot. Define this carefully by using a turning tool against the base of the bowl as it revolves.

7

7 Use a throwing rib to grind a sharp line between the foot and the bowl, emphasizing the form of both. This ensures that the foot will give 'lift' to the bowl. Final smoothing may be done with a credit card, which gives a very precise line.

8

8 The foot has been shaped with three angles. Light falls on the three surfaces with varying intensity, casting shadows, and gives a strong profile to the foot. Remove the knobs of clay, place the bowl upside down on a board and leave it to dry before slipping and biscuiting for decoration.

USING A BAT

If you want to make a particularly large pot, such as a large bowl, you will find that there may be a problem when you want to remove it from the wheel. A large pot will have delicate sides that are likely to cave in if touched. To avoid such a disaster many potters use a bat, a circular board which fits on to the wheel so that the pot can be carried away from the wheel on the bat.

Some wheels have three prongs on to which you can fix a bat. On other wheels it is necessary to provide an anchorage in the form of a series of concentric clay rings to which the bat can adhere.

1

2

3

4

1 To fix a wooden bat to a wheel without prongs first throw a centred piece of clay, then flatten it out exerting pressure with your hands. If your wheel has prongs, then simply fit the bat on them.

2 Make concentric rings with your fingertips, starting from the centre and gradually working outwards across the wheel. Then smooth the sides and tops of the rings with your fingertips. This is to flatten them and provide an even surface to hold the bat in position.

3 Place the bat on the wheel. The concentric rings work like suction pads so that the bat will adhere to the clay on the wheel. Then push the bat down hard on the clay rings. Use a little water while doing this and push right across the bat to make sure it is secure. Unless the bat adheres well it will work loose from the wheel, pushing your pot off-centre and ruining your throwing.

4 Proceed as usual, treating the bat as the wheel.

MAKING A FOOT

An alternative way of making a foot is to turn it from the base of the actual pot itself. This method is often used for large pots, where a coil foot might be more difficult to handle and to secure adequately, and where the shape of a pot dictates that only a shallow foot is suitable. Every potter has their own method of turning a foot and their own particular favoured tools, so do experiment and work out the best way for you. You must always bear in mind, however, the thickness of the clay and the inside shape of the pot so that you do not pare away too much and create thin, weak areas.

1

2

3

4

1 Before starting make a thin line to show where the foot will spring from. Use a turning tool to cut into the base of the bowl to make a vertical edge. Remember to check the thickness of the clay by tapping it as you proceed.

2 A metal turning tool can give a variety of surfaces, depending on the angle at which you hold it. Here the potter is creating a slightly oblique line. It is the angles of the lines that catch the light and shadows to emphasize the form of the foot and so give 'lift' to the pot.

3 A wooden turning tool is used to delineate the division between the foot and the bottom of the bowl — and a deep line sharply throws up the shadow. The foot gives strength and vitality to the pot.

4 Finally, a wooden turning tool is used to smooth the edge of the foot and side of the bowl to give a 'clean' profile. Wooden tools are more 'sympathetic' to clay than metal ones and give a more rounded feel.

CONTROLLING A BRUSH

While all processes in pottery are enjoyable, the area of decoration can sometimes be the greatest fun, allowing you to use your imagination to the full.

Drawing and painting on rounded surfaces involves a slightly different approach to working on canvas or paper. With red earthenware the pot needs to be slipped and biscuited first to provide a background for the paint. With a bowl such as the 'Merlin's' bowl shown here you will find it easier to decorate the inside and rim before painting the outside to avoid smudging.

The rim is probably the most awkward part to paint but this can be solved by placing the bowl on a banding wheel, just letting the brush rest lightly on the rim while the wheel revolves.

Ceramic paints can give some surprising results and change in hue when they have been fired, so it is advisable to experiment with the colours beforehand. Paint should not be applied too thickly or the glaze will not sit on it properly later. This is particularly true of red paints, which can disperse the glaze.

1

2

Colours
Golden Yellow
Jet Black
Coral
Delphinium Blue
Juniper Green
Rosso Orange Red
Purple

1 After the bowl has been slipped and biscuited the potter starts decorating it by tackling the inside first. The design is built up and painted in stages, so a pencil outline is drawn in as a guide. Then the flat body colour of the stars is painted in with a fairly thick brush, being careful not to apply the paint too thickly. The rainbow is painted next, its edges merging together. The stars are outlined in black with a thin brush, giving a sharp contrast to the watery look of the rainbow, and small stars are dotted in. Be careful not to touch the paint while working on the bowl as you could smudge it or brush it off. Keep your brush well loaded with watery colour.

2 After the rainbow has been outlined and some abstract 'clouds' painted in, it is time to paint the rim, first placing the bowl on a banding wheel. The technique of painting a line on a pot with the aid of a banding wheel is basically the same whether you use a broad brush for a rim or a thin brush for a decorative line around the pot. Load your brush with paint, and simply let it rest on the rim as the wheel revolves. Lift the brush when you reach the point where the decoration started. Hold the brush with one hand and turn the wheel with the other to control its speed. Repeat the process if necessary, but be careful not to paint the rim too thickly.

3 Now start decorating the outside of the bowl, holding it by the foot so that the paint does not smudge. The design, which complements the inside of the bowl, is first outlined in pencil as a guide.

4 The stars are painted in with a broad brush, again not too thickly. Lastly, outline the stars in black with a thin brush. When the paint is dry the bowl is ready for glazing and firing.

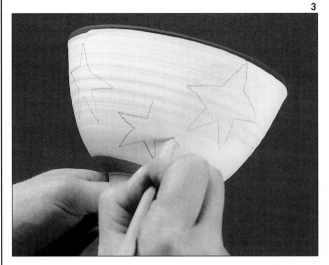

5 The finished glazed 'Merlin's' bowl. Its brightly coloured design complements the form of the pot.

TIPS AND HINTS

Make sure that you wash all your brushes out fully at the end of each session.

Large 'fish' bowl

USING THE WHEEL

This large bowl involves a number of techniques we have looked at. Its size means that it must be thrown on a bat to avoid damaging the bowl when removing it from the wheel. Though large in diameter, however, the bowl is fairly shallow so a strongly defined rim and foot are particularly important to give the bowl an interesting profile. The foot is turned from the base of the bowl itself and care is needed to avoid paring away too much, leaving the base thin and weak.

Such a large area gives ample scope for decoration and here the potter has decided to make the most of the inside of the bowl to paint on a flowing design of fish. The design is built up in stages, using a gradation of tone to give depth. As a contrast the outside of the bowl is left plain and unglazed.

1

Colours
Golden Yellow
Rosso Orange Red
Jet Black
Juniper Green
Tan Brown

1 Secure a bat to the wheel with clay. Then take a large ball of clay — about 2.25kg (5lb) — and tap it down on the wheel. Centre it, bring it up into a cone and then down again to displace any air bubbles. When you are making a large pot such as this it is useful to work out in your mind the sort of shape and possible decoration you want to achieve so that you can plan the building of the pot in stages.

2

2 Start making the base of the bowl by pushing down across the clay with both hands. Be careful not to dig in and make the base too thin — you can check the depth of the base easily by inserting a needle. Make sure you are satisfied with the diameter of the base at this stage as you will not be able to change it once you start building out the sides and profile of the bowl.

3

3 Start bringing out the shape of the bowl with the tips of the fingers of the left hand, while the fingers of the right hand guide the shape. When throwing always try to keep your arms in at your sides so that you have more control. For a bowl you will want to achieve a fairly smooth and lineless surface inside — use a wooden rib or your hands for this.

4

4 Here the potter has built up the shape of the bowl and has pulled up a ring to form a rim. A good depth of clay is required at the top so that you have something to work the rim from. Define the rim with your fingers and smooth it with a sponge. Take care with this part of the potting process — if the rim is not strongly formed it will spoil the look of your bowl.

5 While you are shaping the rim and defining it with a wooden turning tool or whatever tool you prefer, smooth it off with a sponge and then a chamois. All potters have their own methods of working and you will soon find the most suitable for you. The important point to remember is that the division between the rim and the rest of the bowl should be clearly defined and that the rim should be smooth.

6 As the pot is going to be painted inside it is important to check that it is as smooth as possible. Its decoration of wet shiny fish means that this part of the bowl will probably be looked at quite closely when finished. A throwing rib is useful for removing any lines or small bumps from the surface.

5

6

7

7 Lastly, excess clay at the bottom is removed with a wooden turning tool to give it a finer shape. A cheesewire is run underneath the bowl to loosen it from the bat. Twist the bat slightly and remove the bat with the bowl from the wheel. The bowl is now left to dry before placing it upside down on the bat to turn a foot from the base.

8 The bowl has been slipped and biscuited and is now ready for decoration — in this case the image of some golden fish swimming across the bowl. Draw the design in using an ordinary pencil — the carbon will burn off during the firing process. Lay on the body colour of one fish with a fairly broad brush and then paint in the next fish similarly in a slightly different tone. Then outline them in black with a fine brush.

9 Another fish is pencilled in to build up the design. Add shading in a darker tone of paint as appropriate to the colour of the fish and dab it on with a broad brush. The brush must be fairly wet as the biscuited slip is quite absorbent, but do be careful not to apply the paint too thickly or it will cause the glaze to blister when fired.

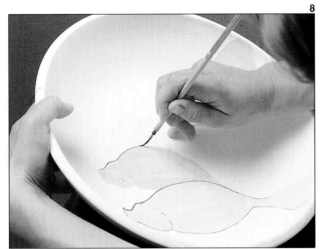

10 You can see clearly here how lighter and darker tones of colour are dabbed in to give depth and shape to the fish. The scales are suggested by crosshatching with a fine brush, and fins painted in.

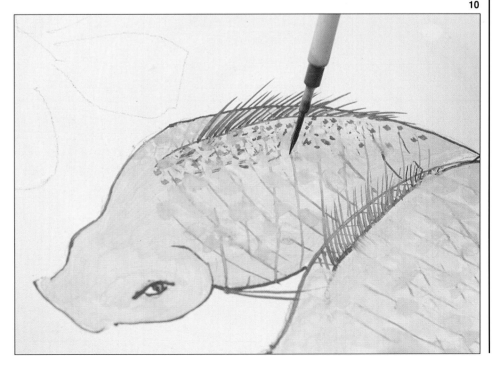

11 To complete the composition the potter painted in a sprig of river weed. This adds a naturalistic touch and introduces a contrasting colour into the bowl.

TIPS AND HINTS

Get your eye in for your brush decoration by practising on a piece of newspaper before starting to decorate your bowl.

12 Note how the tails of the fish have been painted in a free impressionistic manner to give a feeling of movement through water. Also, rather than finishing off the bowl with a heavy rim short outward lines are painted with a fine brush. This breaks up the edge and links in to the colours used for painting the inside of the bowl.

13 The decorated bowl is now ready for glazing and firing. The colours will change slightly and become much richer looking. As a finishing touch the potter has painted her personal mark on the bowl.

14 The glazed 'fish' bowl — a rich display of ceramic art.

Basic techniques

COIL HANDLE

A simple handle for a cup or mug may be made by rolling a coil. This may seem rather unexciting but there are a number of ways in which you can adapt a basic coil to form a handle that is out of the ordinary. Coils may be flattened, incised or impressed with pattern, or twisted, and, of course, they can be moulded to produce a variety of shapes. A handle must be firmly fixed to the cup and comfortable to hold in the hand. It should balance well and look right.

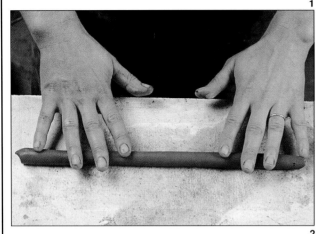

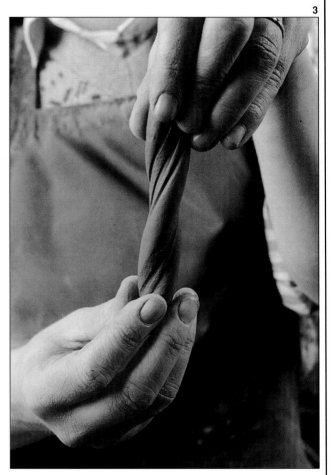

1 Roll a coil of clay. If you are going to make a 'loving cup' it must be long enough for two handles, allowing for the ends which will be joined to the cup. Make sure that the coil is even throughout its length and of a thickness suitable to the cup.

2 You can flatten the coil and, if you wish, impress lines with thin strips of wood along the length of the coil. A knitting needle can also be used to produce this effect. Cut one handle, then place it against the coil to cut another, measuring it to match.

3 To produce an interesting barley-sugar effect simply hold each end of the impressed coil and twist your hands. This type of handle makes an unusual decorative feature.

SPONGING

Some interesting effects can be produced with coloured slip by using sponges to print a pattern. Natural sponges give the best result but you can also use the foam stoppers found in pharmaceutical packaging. Slip may be spattered on with a toothbrush or laid down in a variety of ways with a slip trailer.

1 Have your pots of coloured slip ready before starting your decoration. The patterns here have been printed with a foam stopper cut to make a pattern. Simply draw your design on to the foam and then cut around it so that you have the design in relief. Dip the foam into the slip and press it firmly down on your pot or tile. Further sprays of colour can be overlaid by spattering with a toothbrush. Just dip the brush into the slip and flick the bristles to shower the colour on.

2 Further layers of sponging can be built up over each other.

3 A slip trailer can be used to produce blobs and squiggles to link the different areas of the design and to give it an outline. Make sure that the slip is fairly liquid so that it will not clog in the trailer.

Loving cup

USING THE WHEEL

This 'loving cup' might make a rather unusual and practical gift. The cup is thrown on the wheel and involves a number of techniques we have looked at. Its foot, turned from the base, helps to emphasize the shape of the cup, and its double handles make an interesting decorative feature. Rolled from a simple coil, the handles are flattened, impressed and twisted into a barley-sugar style.

The decoration combines several different approaches. The cup is sponged with a natural sponge to give a pleasing mottled effect. Detail is added on one side in the form of a stamp of clay pressed out with a sprigging tool, and then encircled with a painted spray of flowers. The rim is painted with the aid of a banding wheel.

1

2

Materials
450g (1lb) clay
Turning tools
Sponge
Chamois
Sprigging tool
Cheesewire
Paintbrushes
Banding wheel

Colours
Delphinium Blue
Golden Yellow
Purple
Jet Black

1 Take a small ball of clay and tap it on to the wheel so that it is firm. Then centre the clay. Push with your right hand and guide the clay with your left, holding them together in a squeezing action. If you keep your elbows in you will be able to exert more pressure.

2 Push the clay into a flattish shape with the side of your palm to enable you to begin from the base. Then push your finger down into the centre. Next, draw it across to '3 o'clock' to make the base. The cup is pulled straight up from the base before you start pushing it outwards. Form the shape with your left hand inside the cup.

3

3 Pull a ring up from the base to form a rim. Define its line with your fingernail and then smooth it off with a damp sponge and a chamois.

The rim must be smooth and rounded so that you can drink easily from the cup.

4

4 The foot is formed by pushing in slightly with a wooden turning tool about 1cm (0.5in) from the bottom. This makes the cup look as if it is rising from a good solid base. Support your right hand with your left hand inside the cup during this process. Note how smooth and rounded the rim is.

5

5 The barley-sugar twist handles are added to the cup. Smooth out the clay where they join with your fingertips to make sure they are firmly attached. The stamp is formed by pressing a sprigging tool into a small knob of clay placed on the cup. Crosshatch the cup before putting the knob in position so that it adheres. Peel the tool carefully away to leave a clear impression. The pressing action also helps to fix it firmly.

6 The cup looks strong and interesting. Its rim and foot complement each other as do the barley-sugar twist handles and stamp. Note that the stamp has not been placed too high or the cup would be difficult to drink from. After drying the pot is ready for slipping.

6

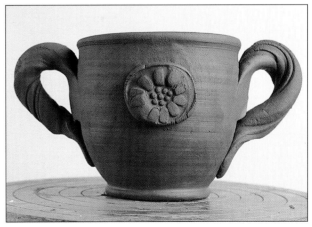

7 The cup is slipped inside by swirling the slip around and pouring the excess back into the slip bucket. When dry, the outside of the cup is slipped. Hold the cup by its foot and immerse it in the slip to within about 2cm (1in) of the base. This also ensures that the rim is well covered. The slip should be the consistency of double cream.

8 Give the cup a little twist in your hand to shake off any excess drops of slip and wipe around the base with a damp sponge if necessary. Check that there are no large drips on the handles.

9 When the slipped cup is dry it is ready for biscuiting. The slip forms a background for further painted decoration.

10 The cup is sponged all over with a small natural sponge to give a mottled background. Use a real sponge for this technique if you can. Dip the sponge into a paint 'wash' and dab it evenly over the surface to avoid a repeat pattern. Hold the cup by the foot to avoid smudging the paint.

11 As a finishing touch the potter is painting in a spray of flowers around the stamp. The stamp itself can also be painted in if you wish. It is important not to add too much paint or you will spoil the overall effect of the shaped decoration. Hold the cup by its foot for these techniques. The rim, however, is painted by placing the cup on a banding wheel, turning it and letting the brush rest upon it.

10

11

12

12 The 'loving cup' after it has been glazed and fired. You could, of course, simply make a cup with one handle following the same method, and there is a variety of decoration that you might like to experiment with.

Chapter 7

Throwing cylinders

Progressing from throwing a bowl on the wheel to throwing cylinder shapes with bases opens up the possibility of making a whole range of useful pots such as jars and jugs.

These types of ware also involve a number of other interesting techniques — for instance, throwing a lid and making it fit the jar, 'pulling' a handle, and shaping a lip so that a jug pours easily. All of these techniques need practice to master them but learning to make pots well accounts for a great deal of the fun of ceramics. Whatever type of clay you use the basic methods are similar, though there may be a slight difference in the feel of the clay as you handle it. Controlling your movements and producing a balanced form is the secret of a pot that looks right and fulfils its function.

In this chapter we take a more detailed look at design — especially at the importance of balancing your decoration so that it enhances the shape of your pot. Avoid over-decoration — if you limit your pattern or colours you will probably achieve a more satisfying result. Take your time to plan your decoration, and think about unusual finishing touches.

Basic techniques

CORRECTING AN UNEVEN TOP

Even when you have learnt to throw properly and can produce a pot with a satisfying shape inevitably you will make the odd mistake. A common problem is to spoil the pot just as you are finishing it or to knock the rim accidentally. Do not despair — you can easily rectify the error by cutting around the top with a cheesewire. Simply lift off the excess piece of clay, then reshape and smooth the rim.

1 This pot has unfortunately been knocked out of shape at the top. The clay is thin in this area and accidents can easily happen.

2 Even off the top of the pot by cutting through the clay with a cheesewire. Do not just slice straight across the pot but work carefully around the edge. Occasionally you may also find some air bubbles on your pot that have not been worked out in the centring process. Simply prick these with a needle and smooth the clay.

3 Remove the excess strip of clay from the pot. Then reshape the rim and smooth it off with a wet chamois. Odd pieces of clay can be combined with other clay to be reused later.

SHAPING A LIP

A good jug pours easily and does not drip. The technique of making a lip is not difficult but does need extra care as the clay around the rim of a jug is very thin. Your movements need to be deft and positive or you can easily knock the lip out of shape. The lip is formed by gently pulling up the clay, then shaping the spout by pinching the rim in and moulding it with the end of your finger and knuckle.

1

2

1 Wet your fingers and then, using your index finger and thumb, gently pull up the clay. This part of the rim will stand up a little higher than the rest.

2 Gently smooth the edge of the raised clay with a wet chamois. The clay is now much thinner so you need to do this very carefully.

3 Now shape the lip from inside the jug with the knuckle and end of your index finger. At the same time pinch the rim from outside the jug with the thumb and index finger of your other hand.

3

PULLING A HANDLE

The handle of a jug must balance well so that it not only supports the pot but is also comfortable to hold when pouring. So you need to use enough clay to provide a firm and generous-looking handle. A traditional jug has a 'pulled' handle. The technique described here involves pulling a piece of clay, then flattening and shaping it with your hand. The ends are neatly tapered by severing them between your fingers with a scissors action. It is also possible to pull a knob of clay from the pot itself to form a handle, as many potters do.

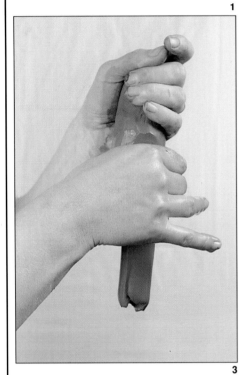

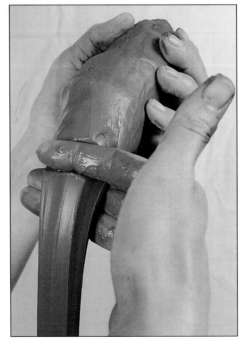

1 Hold a generous piece of clay in one hand and shape it with the other, keeping it at eye level. Use downward movements, pulling the clay between your thumb and whole hand into a flattish shape. Wet your pulling hand for this process so that the clay does not stick.

2 Pulling the handle should be a continuous smooth and controlled action. Strike down at the edges to flatten and shape the sides of the handle. Use your fingers in a scissors movement to nip off the end bit of clay. This avoids jagged edges and should be done whenever necessary during the pulling process to tidy up the handle.

3 Define the shape of the handle by making two indentations at the top with the tips of your index finger and thumb. Continue the lines down and continue pulling and stretching the handle.

4 When you are happy with the shape of the handle nip off the top at the opposite angle to that at the bottom. This picture shows clearly the scissors action required by the first two fingers.

5 Bend the top of the handle away from you and place it on a board. Guide the handle into a natural curve and then leave it to harden before attaching it to the jug.

6 Place the jug on a banding wheel. Crosshatch with a modelling tool or knife where the handle is to be joined to the jug. Dab a tiny bit of slip on to the scraped patch — this will help the two pieces of clay to adhere. Then press the handle on to the jug, squeezing between your thumb and fingers. Hold the handle out with your other hand while you press firmly.

7 Smooth the handle on to the jug at the top with your fingers. Then press the bottom part of the handle on in the same way, flattening with your thumb. You do not need to crosshatch here, however, as there is not such a great amount of clay to join. Smooth off with your fingers. You can use a sponge to clean away excess clay.

8 The handle seems to 'spring' from the jug, giving the pot life. The jug is now ready to be slipped and biscuit fired prior to painting if you wish.

5

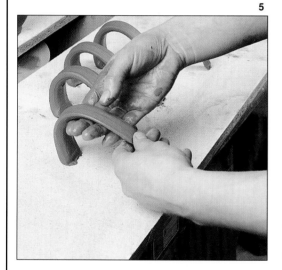

6

7

8

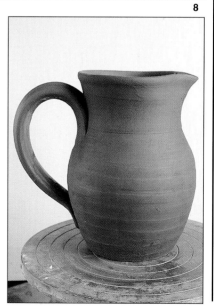

BALANCING A DESIGN

When you are painting the outside of a curved pot such as a jug or jar you need to make sure that the design is evenly balanced.

This involves looking at your pot from various angles to check that some areas are not being given less or more attention than others. A sensible approach is to build up the design gradually.

With abstract decoration this may mean placing the broad flowing strokes and swirls first, linking their shapes with thin lines.

With a more precise design such as a striped jug the method is similar — the broad strokes of one colour are painted in downwards first before adding further lines.

Colours should also balance. If you don't have much experience of using colour limit the number you use on a pot until you have more confidence. Mistakes can be removed if you wipe the paint off immediately with a damp sponge.

1

2

1 Underglaze colours come in powder form, so are mixed up with water, then applied as a wash — a piece of glass makes a useful palette for mixing. The colours change slightly in firing, but experience will soon enable you to select the correct tones you wish. Here the potter is applying Delphinium Blue using a broad brush with a free-flowing stroke.

2 Turn the jug in your hand so that you can balance the design. Here, Juniper Green is being painted on.

3 A third colour, Golden Yellow, is added.

3

4 The potter has complemented the design of broad brush strokes with Jet Black lines painted on with a thin brush. Colours used on the jug are also used for a broad band down the handle and for the rim. It is a good idea to limit the number of colours you use or the design can lose its impact. The rim colour is applied by placing the jug on a banding wheel, then letting the loaded brush rest on the rim as the wheel revolves.

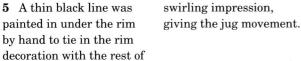

6 The abstract design is balanced and complemented on the other side of the jug.

5 A thin black line was painted in under the rim by hand to tie in the rim decoration with the rest of the jug. Notice how the black lines do not follow the coloured shapes exactly, but create a swirling impression, giving the jug movement.

7 With this striped jug the stripes were painted downwards from the neck line. Broad stripes of Cobalt Blue were painted in first, then of Juniper Green, before finally filling in with thin lines of Jet Black. Leaving the neck of the jug white provides a contrast. The rim and the thin black line around the neck were painted in last on the banding wheel.

Striped jug
THROWING CYLINDERS

Throwing a traditional jug is a challenge to any potter, and the secret of making a successful jug is to pull together all the key elements with control and balance.

In the jug demonstrated in this project the cylinder shape has to be controlled before bellying out to form the body of the jug. The neck is curved inwards and then flares out at the top — this leaves an area of very thin clay around the rim which can easily be damaged if you are not careful. The lip is pinched out with gentle, positive movements — it needs to be well smoothed and finely moulded so that the jug pours properly and does not drip.

The handle is pulled from a piece of clay. As with the lip, there is a variety of methods of providing a handle. In this case a pulled handle allows you to achieve the correct balance for the shape of the jug before you attach it. This area of the jug must be strong both visually and practically. If the handle cannot support the jug when full then the pot is of little use.

Decorating a jug also involves control and balance because, unless you have decided to paint one side only, you have to ensure that the design is equally distributed around the surface. If you are painting the decoration it is as well to limit the number of colours you use — knowing when to stop gives the design a chance to complement the form of the jug rather than swamping it. In the jug featured here only two colours are used. The underglaze colours are applied to the body of the jug as a wash with broad and thin brush strokes in a stripes and dots design. The neck is left white as a contrast to the coloured pattern, and neatly delineated with a thin black line.

Materials
700g (1lb 8oz) clay
Turning tools
Throwing rib
Sponge
Chamois
Paintbrushes
Banding wheel

Colours
Rosso Orange Red
Jet Black

1 To make a jug or jar you need to throw a cylinder shape with a base. First centre the clay, coning it to remove all the air bubbles. When you have brought the clay down to a flattish shape start making the base by pushing your right-hand fingers into the centre of the clay. The left hand guides the piece of clay in.

Make the base slightly wider than you need for the jug as the clay will start to move in as you form the cylinder.

2 Pull across the base and make a little ridge inside with your left-hand fingers, while the right hand controls the clay. This gives a point from which you can bring up your cylinder. It is important not to use too much water, otherwise the pot becomes 'tired.'

3

3 With one hand inside the clay at the top and the other outside at the bottom, make a small indentation around the outside. Pull the clay up from here to start forming the cylinder. Use a sponge, or knuckle, on the outside to exert gentle extra pressure.

4

5

6

4 Pull the clay up into a cone, being careful not to let the cylinder flare out at the top. The widest part should always be at the bottom.

5 Make the belly of the jug by pushing out with your left hand from inside the pot.

6 When you have shaped the belly of the jug, let the top part of the cylinder continue straight up to form the neck.

TIPS AND HINTS

When throwing, handle the clay firmly but gently. You must exert positive control over the clay.

7 The top of the belly of the pot is carefully curved in to the straight neck. Form the rim with the tip of your right finger pressed gently against the clay.

8 Smooth the pot and put in a line around the neck with a throwing rib. This accentuates the parts of the pot and defines the shape. Smooth the rim off with a wet chamois. You now have the choice of leaving the pot as a jar, as illustrated on the cover, or giving it a lip and handle to make a jug.

9 The lip is formed by gently pulling up the clay between your index finger and thumb. Shape it with the knuckle of your index finger and a pinching movement.

10 Shape the bottom of the jug with a wooden turning tool. This gives a nice rounded shape so that the form seems to 'rise'. Smooth off, then clean inside with a sponge. Remove the jug from the wheel by passing a cheesewire underneath, and leave it to harden. When the jug is nearly dry you can attach the handle.

11 When slipping the jug you should hold it by the foot, not the handle. Having done the inside (ladling slip into the jug and then shaking it as you turn it upside down to pour it round, out and over the rim — wiping off any drips with a damp sponge), followed by the rim and neck (plunging the pot into the slip, holding it by the foot) you then slip the outside. Place your hands inside to hold it and plunge it into the bucket of slip.

12 The jug is plunged into the slip right up to the rim so that it is completely covered. The slip should be the consistency of double cream.

11

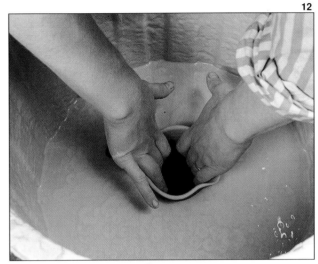

12

13

13 Give the jug a smooth twist as you remove it from the slip. Start by the handle so that if the slip does form blobs and drips they will be on the sides. Wipe off the base of the jug with a damp sponge. The jug is now ready for biscuit firing prior to painting.

TIPS AND HINTS

Sometimes the edges of a pot feel rather rough after biscuit firing, but they can be rubbed down with sandpaper.

14 Underglaze colours are used to paint the striped jug. They are available in powder form and are mixed with water to make a wash. Use a piece of glass for a palette — this enables you to see the colours clearly and it can be easily cleaned afterwards. The first stripes are painted on in Rosso Orange Red using a broad brush. Paint downwards holding the jug in your hand so that you can control the brush. Do not apply the paint too thickly or it will repel the glaze in the firing process.

15 Jet Black lines are painted in downwards with a thin brush to outline the broad strokes.

14

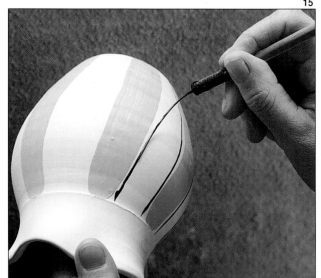

15

16 To strengthen the form of the jug a thin black line is painted around the neck. This line gives the pot 'tension' and clearly defines the division between the parts of the jug, highlighting the patterned area. It is painted by placing the jug on a banding wheel, resting the brush against it and then turning the wheel. Keep your eyes level with the jug while doing this, and support your elbow.

16

17 As a contrast to the stripes Rosso Orange Red dots are dabbed on to the white areas. Be careful when handling the jug while you are painting as you can easily rub the paint off or leave fingermarks. Equally, however, if you make a mistake or change your mind you can wipe the paint off with a damp sponge.

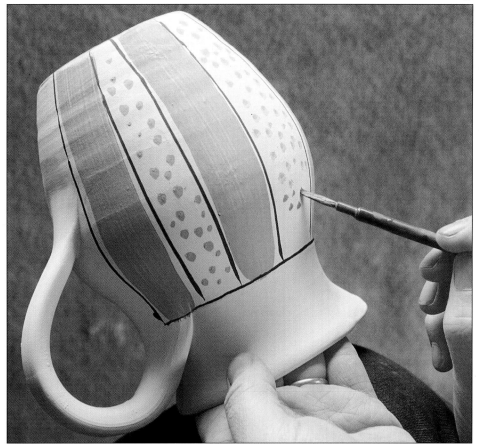

18 Black dots are then painted in to complete the pattern on the body of the jug. Finally, the rim is painted with Rosso Orange Red, by placing it on a banding wheel. Make sure the brush is well loaded with paint, but is not applied too thickly.

TIPS AND HINTS

If you find that a strong red or blue colour is difficult to apply, mix in a little milk.

19 The body of the jug is glazed first. Hold the jug inside and then dip it into the glaze up to the neck. This avoids the problem of touching the painted decoration which can be easily damaged until protected.

20 As you remove the pot from the glaze shake and twist it gently to lose any excess and drips. Wipe the base off with a damp sponge — do this immediately, before the glaze can dry. Leave the jug to dry for a minute or two.

21 Glaze the inside of the jug by pouring the glaze in with a ladle. Swill it around, then hold the pot upside down to pour the excess back into the glaze bucket, giving it a twist as you do so. Allow the glaze to dry, then hold the jug upside down and dip it in the glaze to cover the neck. Give it a gentle twist and shake as you remove it.

TIPS AND HINTS

When it has dried, any lines or globules in the glaze can be smoothed over with your fingertips before putting the pot in the kiln to fire.

22 After firing, with the decoration now protected by a glassy finish. The stripes give an impression of formal design, yet they have been applied in a free-flowing style. This 'softness' contrasts well with the strength of the form of the jug.

22

Porcelain ginger jar

THROWING CYLINDERS

The beauty of porcelain is its whiteness and translucence, the latter being due to the presence of materials such as potash and feldspar which help it melt in firing. These are coarse-grained so porcelain 'wets up' quickly, and when fired it becomes very hard.

Working with porcelain needs a slightly different approach as it has a 'memory' and the clay tends to carry on moving in the direction it has been thrown in, twisting slightly in the firing.

The traditional ginger jar shown in this project is a good introduction to getting a feel for porcelain. It involves throwing a cylinder, bellying it out to shape the body of the jar, and turning the base from inside to form the foot. The lid, measured to fit, is thrown separately and also turned inside.

Coloured slip is used to decorate the jar, with a carefully balanced sgraffito design scratched out of it. A wax-resist method is used to prevent slip or glaze adhering to areas such as the bottom of the jar or around the lid. The jar is finished with a fine gold band.

Materials	Ruler
700g (1lb 8oz) clay (jar)	Measuring collar
	Latex
150g (4oz) clay (lid)	Cheesewire
Turning tools	Pencil
Modelling tools	Paintbrush
Throwing hook	
Potter's pin	
Sponge on stick	
Chamois	

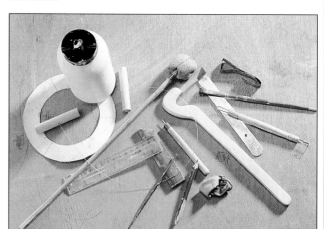

2

1

1 Make the jar first. Wet your hands — you should always remember to keep a bowl of water nearby. Then centre the clay on the wheel, coning it up and bringing it down as usual to remove the air bubbles. Bring the clay down to a flattish dome shape to start forming the jar.

2 Cup your hands around the clay to support and guide the beginnings of the pot. Move your thumb into the centre to start making the jar. You will find the feel of porcelain different to that of earthenware or stoneware, but practice will enable you to control it just as well. A foot ring is going to be turned from the bottom of this jar, so remember to leave a thicker base.

3 Pull up the clay between the tips of your fingers and the thumb of your left hand, guiding the clay with your right-hand fingertips, to form a cylinder. Continue to pull clay up from the bottom until the cylinder has reached the height needed for the jar.

4 When the cylinder is of a reasonable height start bellying out the jar with the fingers of your left hand inside the pot. Guide the shape with your right hand on the outside. Push the clay in slightly at the top where the rim will be.

5 The left hand is now able to get right inside the pot to produce the rounded shape required for the jar.

3

5

4

6

7

6 Once the jar has been bellied out to a satisfactory shape the first guiding line for the rim can be put in place. This is simply done with your thumb nail.

7 You can also use a throwing hook to hollow out the shape of the jar where it starts getting difficult to move your hand inside. Smooth the inside with a sponge. The throwing hook also helps the smoothing process. Then measure the diameter of the rim of the pot so that you will have an idea of how big to make the lid.

TIPS AND HINTS

Do make sure that the rim is strong to avoid the possibility of chipping at a later stage.

8

9

10

8 Smooth off the edge of the jar with a wooden turning rib. Hold the tool at a slight angle to follow the line of the curve on the pot.

9 Trim off the base of the jar with the wooden turning rib. You can easily make your own tools for this sort of job — this one is simply made from metal strapping.

10 Now trim off the rim to give a vertical edge. By now the pot may have collected quite a bit of water from sponges and your hands. Place a sponge on a stick inside the jar to absorb this. Chamois around the rim to smooth off. Then pass a cheesewire under the base and remove the pot to dry.

11 The lid for the ginger jar is also thrown on the wheel. After centring and coning to remove air bubbles the clay is pushed down and flattened with the side of the hand.

12 To make the lid the clay is pulled out into a dish shape. This is done by placing your fingertips in the clay and drawing them across, supporting the shape with your left thumb outside the rim. Having measured the rim of the jar with calipers or a ruler, measure the lid so that you know it will fit on the jar. It should be slightly larger (a millimetre or two) than the rim so that it fits snugly but will not stick.

11

12

13

13 Smooth and shape the base of the lid with a metal turning tool. Soft clays, especially porcelain, can sometimes crack when fired. By smoothing over frequently you compress the clay a bit more, and this helps to avoid the problem. Chamois around the edge of the lid to smooth it and then leave it to dry.

14

15

16

14 When the jar is dry — usually within twenty-four hours — you can start turning the foot ring. Place the pot upside down on the wheel, check it is in the centre and put coils of clay around it to hold it. Press the clay down so that the pot is quite secure. Then trim off the edge of the base with a metal loop turning tool. Follow the shape of the jar around the base to give a gentle curve and flatten the bottom edge off.

15 The centre of the base is scooped out with the same tool. Work from the centre out to make the correct shape so that the base is indented and slopes gently down at the edges. The clay is removed in spirals with this tool and it is easy to get carried away — so be careful not to pare too much.

17

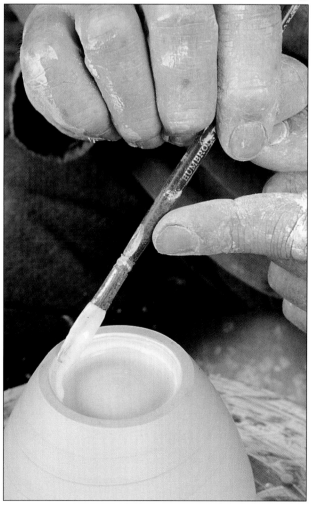

16 When the lid has dried this is also gently turned away to produce a neat edge and slightly domed top. Place the lid on the wheel right side up and make sure that it is as near as possible in the centre. A little water on the wheel may help you secure the lid. Work from the centre outwards.

17 The pot is going to be slipped and later glazed so a wax-resist technique is used to repel these substances from the jar in areas where they are not wanted. Latex is painted on to the base and bottom edge of the jar. It can be peeled off later. Make sure you wash your brush immediately if you want it to last.

Recipe for blue slip
1kg (2lb 2oz) ball clay
50g (2oz) red iron oxide
50g (2oz) managanese
dioxide
50g (2oz) cobalt oxide

18 Paint latex on to the rim of the lid to avoid the slip adhering to it. The lid is then dipped in dark blue slip. Hold it upside down with your fingertips inside exerting outward pressure. As you remove it

shake it slightly to remove any excess. Wipe off any odd dribbles with a damp sponge.

19 The wax-resist technique ensures a nice sharp line between the blue slip and natural porcelain. This defines the rim.

18

19

20

21

20 The jar itself is slipped in a similar fashion. Hold it inside with your fingers exerting an outward pressure and then dip the pot into the slip to just beneath the rim where you have painted on latex. Shake the jar slightly as you take it out. Again, any drips can be removed with a sponge.

21 The slipped pot and lid. When the latex has been removed areas of natural porcelain will contrast well with the dark blue of the jar.

22 When the slip is dry you can remove the latex. Simply peel it away using a sharp pointed tool to reveal a clear division between the coloured slip and the natural porcelain. This wax-resist technique can, of course, be used on any type of clay and for a variety of decorative effects.

22

23 This jar is going to be decorated with a sgraffito technique. To balance the design around the jar use a home-made paper collar to measure around the neck. This one is sectioned off into thirds. At each of the three lines on the collar the potter puts a pencil mark on the jar to show where the decoration will be placed.

23

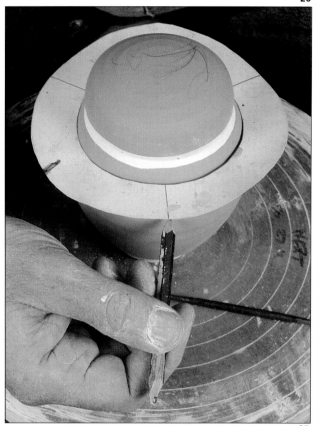

24

24 Sgraffito involves incising the top layer of slip so that the white clay underneath shows through. The design here is based on fuchsias. First draw your design in pencil as a guide. Then scrape over the outline with a sharp metal pointed tool — special sgraffito tools are available. Finish by scratching out the central part of the design. It is advisable to wear a face mask for this process to avoid breathing in the dust.

25

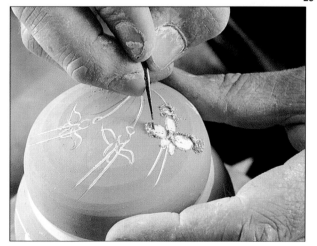

25 The lid is also decorated with fuchsias incised in sgraffito. Here, the central part is being scraped away — note the amount of dust created. It is a good idea to decorate the pot before the lid so that the lid can tie the whole design together. Some potters also incise a design or their initials or mark underneath the pot inside the foot ring.

26

26 After biscuit firing the jar is ready to be glazed. Again, use the wax-resist technique of applying latex to the areas where you do not want the glaze to adhere — the natural porcelain rim and top part of the neck, the base of the jar, and the rim of the lid.

27 A small jar like this

27 A small jar like this can easily be held in one hand and dipped into the glaze in one go. Make sure that the glaze covers the pot completely inside and out.

27

28

29

28 The jar is taken out of the glaze completely covered. Pour the glaze out from the inside and remove any drips.

29 The jar is fired at 1280°C (2330°F). Then a fine gold line is painted around the neck and fired at 830°C (1530°F).

30 A traditional ginger jar. The dark blue slip contrasts with the natural porcelain colour which shows through the sgraffito decoration. The graceful fuchsias complement the curve of the jar and the gold band gives a smart finish.

Chapter 8
Combining shapes

We have now looked at the basic shapes that you can make on the wheel and it is time to look at pots that may not appear to be quite so straightforward. However, pots which seem to be of complicated design can sometimes be simpler to make than you think. Often it is a matter of analysing the components that make up a form, producing them separately and joining them together. They may require some planning, and quite likely entail some measuring so that pieces fit together accurately.

While the plate, introduced in the cheese bell project in this chapter, is a shape you have not met before, you have already practised the skills required. The real challenge here is in producing the bowl to the correct size, and then decorating the two components so that they form a unit, with a common theme on a flat and curved surface.

Finally, we look at combining shapes in another type of clay — raku — which uses a rather different approach to making a teapot. It is a coarse-grained clay that must be low fired. By its very nature raku has enormous possibilities for imaginative glazing and firing techniques.

Basic techniques

THROWING A PLATE

Making a plate involves a great deal of control. The plate must be flat, and thick enough to support whatever it is to be used for, but not so thick that it is heavy or clumsy. It usually needs some kind of a rim, again depending on the use to which it will be put. It is advisable to throw a plate on a bat so that you do not distort the shape when removing it from the wheel. The plate shown on these pages is specifically designed to accompany the cheese bell project we shall be looking at next. It has a fairly high rim so that the bowl of the cheese bell can fit inside. Its diameter is also carefully measured against the bowl, both inside and out, so that the two match for size.

Finally, the plate is turned at a slight angle at the base to give the form a 'lift'. A nice even finish is achieved by smoothing off with a credit card.

Materials

1kg (2lb 4oz) clay
Bat
Turning tools
Throwing rib
Credit card
Potter's pin

1 Place a bat on the wheel, anchoring it with concentric rings of clay. Make sure that the bat is wet, then centre the clay for the plate, coning it up and down to remove any air bubbles. Making a plate is similar to making a base except that you work right across the clay. Push across with your left hand, steadying it with your right hand on top. Work into the rim with the tips of your fingers.

2 Now put your whole left palm flat upon the clay to shape the plate. Use a throwing rib to smooth the surface. Measure the inside diameter of the rim with calipers. This is essential if you are making a plate to match the cheese bell, and also important if you are making a set of plates which should all be the same size — remember to allow for shrinkage in the firing process. You can judge the thickness of the plate by feel — something that will come with experience or you can tell more precisely by inserting a needle into the clay.

3

3 Smooth the plate with a throwing rib or a credit card. Check the inside diameter with calipers.

4

4 Trim the side and bottom of the plate with a wooden turning tool to produce a finished edge. By giving the plate a slight angle the form seems to 'lift' so that the plate looks less solid.

5

5 Finally, form the rim with the edge of your index finger, shaping it gently between the second finger and thumb of your other hand. With the wheel stopped, use a long cheesewire to cut the plate from the board. Remove the plate from the bat to dry.

Cheese bell

COMBINING SHAPES

The technique for making this cheese bell is more straightforward than you might think. You will find it easier to throw the bowl first, before making the plate to fit it, measuring carefully so that they are a complete match.

The bowl has a coiled and shaped handle, and both the bowl and plate are decorated with the same flower theme. The paint is applied in varying density.

Materials
1.25kg (2lb 12oz) clay
Turning tools
Sponge
Chamois
Cheesewire
Hole cutter

Colours
Coral
Slate Blue
Cobalt Blue
Juniper Green
Grass Green

1 Throw the bowl outwards, making the shape as you go by pulling with your right hand. Your left hand forms the bowl from inside and keeps it bellied, but it is the right hand that controls the shape. Start forming a rim by pulling a ring of clay to the top.

2 Shape the base of the bowl gently with a wooden turning tool. You do not need to make a foot as you would when making an ordinary bowl. This part, which will form the top of the cheese bell, will be rounded off by paring away at a later stage, so make sure you leave enough clay to round off.

3 The rim is shaped by gently pressing the edge of the bowl between your thumb and second finger. Form a ledge with the tip of the index finger of your other hand from inside the bowl. The top should be fairly flat as it must rest upside down on the plate when the cheese bell is complete.

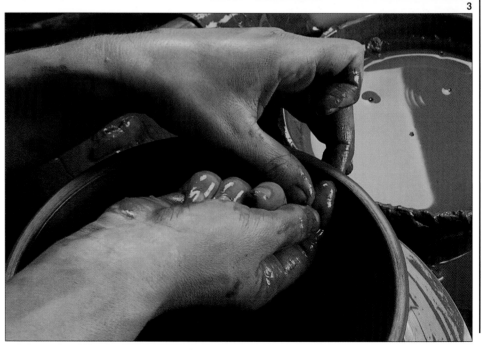

4 When you are happy with the shape and rim of the bowl smooth it off. Cut it underneath with a cheesewire and slide the bowl off the wheel. Leave it to harden.

5 When the bowl is leather hard — dry enough to move, but still soft enough to work on with a tool — place it upside down on the wheel. Press knobs of clay down around it to secure it. Then turn away with a metal tool to produce a domed shape. Check that you are not cutting the clay too thinly by tapping the bowl — the higher the sound the thinner the clay. Smooth off the bowl with a credit card or wooden throwing rib.

6 The handle on this bell is made by rolling a coil. The potter made some grooves in it as decoration and then slapped the coil against a board to flatten it. It is twisted when joined to the bowl. Try the handle on the bell first to check that it is the right length and that the style suits it.

7 With a pointed tool crosshatch the areas on the bowl where the handle will be joined. Add a little slip to the crosshatched areas and press the ends of the handle down firmly, smoothing it in with your fingers. Take care because the clay on the bell is quite thin at the top. Finally, remember to bore a hole through the top so that the cheese will be able to breathe.

4

5

6

7

8

9

10

11

8 Both the bell and plate are slipped to provide a white background for painted decoration. The bell is held upside down, dipped into the slip and removed with a twist to avoid getting slip inside. Ladle the slip onto the plate, shake it around and pour off the excess. Then wipe off the rim and edge with a damp sponge. When the slip is biscuited you can begin painting on it. Here the potter has chosen flowers.

9 The carnation petals are painted on in Coral in sweeping strokes with a broad flat brush. Build up the layers of your decoration, and try to place your brush rather than drawing with it. Use a number of brushes in different ways — try using the side, for instance. Here, the leaves are being painted on, sometimes sweeping right over the petals to give a naturalistic effect.

10 Other flowers are added to follow the curve of the plate. Get into the habit of observing your subject so that you can create the impression of what it is you are trying to paint. It is helpful to concentrate on just one subject so that you have some confidence. Any mistakes can be wiped off with a damp sponge.

11 Decorate the bell in the same way as the plate after it has been biscuited. Finally, glaze them both, but leave the inside of the bell without glaze to allow the cheese to breathe.

TIPS AND HINTS

Place a piece of sponge in the hole when slipping so that the glaze does not run into the inside of the bell.

12 & 13 The finished cheese bell with its unusual twisted handle looks attractive from all angles. The design is well suited to the curved surface, and the colours have taken on a richer hue under the glaze. Notice that the potter has used a limited palette to maximum effect.

Basic techniques

RAKU SLAB DISH

Raku is a low-firing clay which contains a lot of grog. As it is such a coarse-grained clay pots made from it have an open-textured finish. They are usually made with a fairly simple design since any sharp angles tend to produce areas of weakness in the firing.

Decoration is usually in the form of glazes. Again, because of its method of firing, the results are rather unpredictable, and the pots can be fired over and over again to give different and spectacular effects.

This simple slab dish, which could be used for any number of purposes, is moulded over a wooden former.

Materials
Canvas
Rolling pin
Former
Bat
Potter's knife

1 Cover the table with material so that the clay will not stick — something like a piece of old canvas is ideal. Pat out a ball of clay between the palms of your hands. Then roll it out between two pieces of wood so that the slab is even. Roll it into a squarish or rectangular shape depending on the shape of the dish you wish to make. Raku can be moulded as any other clay. Here the potter is using a wooden former that he has specially made for the purpose. Lift the slab and place the former carefully in position.

2 Hold the slab with the former in position in one hand and place a wooden bat on top.

3 Now reverse the bat and clay between the palms of your hands so that your hand is pressing the clay onto the former.

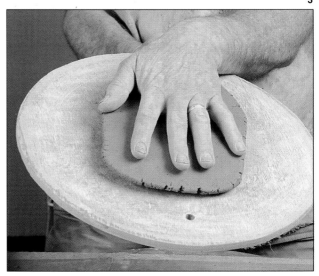

4

5

6

4 Make sure that the former impresses clean, defined corners by tapping the bat with a rolling pin from underneath. The clay will flop into shape over the edges.

5 Place the bat with the clay still on it on the table. Tidy up the edges of the dish with a sharp potter's knife. Do not slice parallel to the lines of the former, but cut at a slight angle to make the dish look more interesting. Turn the dish the right way round and tap on the corners of the former — this gives the corners a bit more 'lift' and strength. Then remove the former.

6 As a finishing touch impress the former sideways to the edge to make a crease in the clay. Now leave the dish to harden before glazing and firing in a raku kiln.

THROWING A LID

The drop-in lid shown here is designed to go with the teapot in the next project. There are many types of lid and every potter has his or her own method of making them. The important point about making a teapot lid, however, is that it should not fall out when the teapot is poured. The lid is usually made first as it is easier to make the top of the teapot to size so that they fit each other properly.

This lid is made by shaping the top of a hump of clay and then cutting it off. The style may also be useful for other jars.

Materials
Bamboo turning tool with string
Throwing rib
Hole cutter

1 Centre the clay by coning. Then build the clay up again into a cone. Start pressing it down to flatten it with your right hand. Hold your left index finger against the clay, and push down, making an indentation. This is the start of the rim. At the same time you will see the knob starting to form at the top.

2 Make the shape of the rim by keeping the second finger of your left hand underneath it. Meanwhile start shaping the top above the rim with your thumbs and index fingers.

3 The sloping part beneath the rim is formed with the tip of your index finger, gently guiding the clay into shape. Use the tips of your fingers of the other hand to make a small well around the knob. Shaping a lid needs co-ordination, but you will find that this comes with practice and experience.

4 Use a throwing rib to smooth off the profile of the lid. Then slightly roll down the edge of the rim on to the wooden tool so that it is flat. This shaping allows the lid to rest neatly in the opening of the teapot.

5 Pinch in the neck of the lid with your thumbs and index fingers. Then incise a line with a bamboo turning tool. Lay a twisted string on the shoulder of the clay and it will automatically start moving into the groove to cut it.

6 Take the lid off the clay with your fingers in a scissors movement, holding it while the string is cutting through. Make sure that the wheel is revolving fairly slowly so that you can control and co-ordinate these actions without the lid toppling over. Finally, when the clay is leather hard, bore a hole through the lid from the top to the bottom to allow steam to escape from the teapot. Smooth off the bottom of the lid with a file.

Raku teapot

COMBINING SHAPES

This teapot is made from raku clay and fired in a raku kiln, but a similar-looking pot could be made from any grogged or coarse-grained stoneware. The various components of the teapot are made separately, and fitted together.

The main body of the pot is thrown first, the opening being measured to fit the lid which has already been made. To avoid throwing a ledge to hold the lid in place, a technique which needs some experience, a coil of clay is added to hold the lid in position when pouring. There are several ways of doing this. Here, the coil is pressed down on to the teapot with the thumb but it could also be thrown up from the teapot if you prefer. The spout is made by rolling a slab of clay and then cutting it to shape around a paper cone. Finally, clay lugs are put on the teapot and a cane handle attached to them.

The teapot is glazed with a white crackle glaze before being fired in a raku kiln.

Materials
1kg (2lb 4oz) clay
Metal turning tools
Wooden modelling tools
Bamboo tool with string
Potter's pin
Cutters for lugs
Hole cutters
Toothbrush
Sponge
Calipers
Paper cone

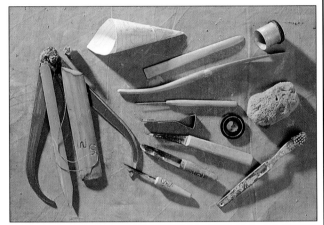

1 Centre the clay, coning it up and down. It is important to have control of the wheel while building the shape of the teapot. It should be revolving fairly fast for centring, but do slow it down if you find you are having difficulty. Use your left hand to control the clay, while your right hand acts as a brace. Start making the shape of the pot by opening the clay into a bowl. Then, with the fingers of your right hand inside the pot and your thumb outside, curve your thumb up under the clay and bring it up, tapering the shape slightly inwards.

2 Put the whole of your left hand inside the pot and lift the clay, guiding it into a sphere. Shape it with the fingers of your right hand from the outside. Continue to do this until you are happy with the profile of the teapot. The wheel should revolve more slowly as you belly out the pot.

3 With your fingertips, 'collar in' where the lid is to fit — using your little finger lean the clay over rather than pushing it in. The wheel should now be revolving at a faster speed. Measure the diameter of the top with calipers to check that it matches the lid you have made. If you are unfortunate enough to find any air bubbles on your thrown pot just prick them with a needle. Smooth off the inside of the teapot with a sponge.

4 Place the lid on the teapot. Crosshatch the shoulder of the pot by rubbing it with a wet toothbrush so that the coil of clay can adhere. Wrap the coil of clay around the pot, pushing it down as you do so. This provides a supporting ledge for the lid so that it will not fall out when the teapot is poured. Cut the height and make the top even if necessary. Smooth the inside of the coil into the top of the ledge with a wooden modelling tool, and a sponge. Use the square end of a turning tool to make the inner edge of the recess stand up straight.

5 Finish off the coil and make sure it is firm. You can do this decoratively by pressing it down with your thumb to leave a pattern, or by smoothing it off with a turning tool. If you wish, you can also add a small protruding 'button' of clay at the top of the ledge to make sure that the lid is safely held in place. This should be fairly wet — just place it on the edge and press it down in the centre with a wooden handle.

6 To make the spout, roll out an even slab of clay. Cut it with a sharp potter's knife curved at one end to allow for fitting the spout against the pot. Then place the paper cone in the centre and wrap the slab around it.

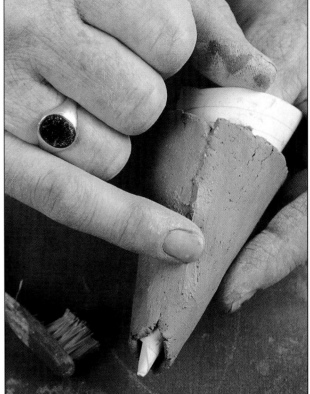

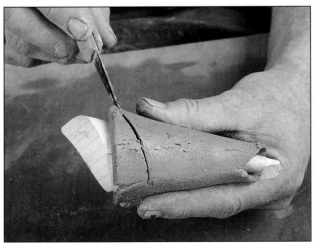

7 Tidy up the two joining edges of the spout with a potter's knife. Crosshatch them with a wet toothbrush, place them together and smooth over the join with a wooden modelling tool and your fingertips.

8 Cut away the spout at an angle, leaving an extra amount of clay at the top for joining on to the teapot.

9 Raise the top edge of the spout to join on to the teapot.

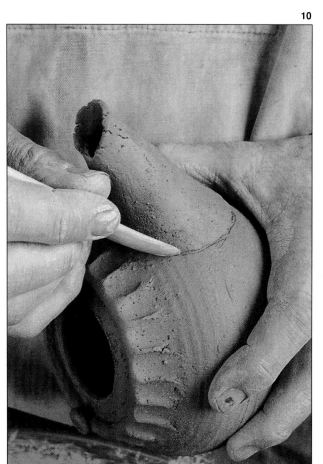

10 Place the spout in position on the teapot, and draw around it with a modelling tool to indicate the outline of the rose. Make sure the top of the spout will be above the level of liquid in the pot.

11 Bore holes for the rose with a hole cutter — pushing the tool first, then twisting. Blow through the holes as you make them to clear away any bits of clay.

12 Scratch the surface around the rose with a wet toothbrush. Wet the surface of the spout and join it to the teapot.

13

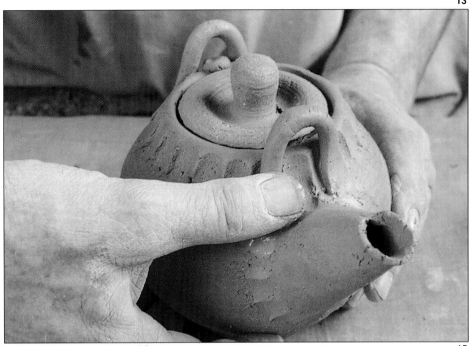

13 Heel the spout well in with your thumb. Smooth around the inner edge of the spout and bend the tip down slightly so that it will pour efficiently. The thinner and sharper the spout the more efficient, but it may also be broken more easily, so you need to compromise. This teapot is going to have a cane handle so two lugs of coiled clay are added, one behind the spout and the other immediately opposite. These are attached in a similar way to the spout, by scratching the edges with a wet toothbrush and then smoothing in.

14

14 The potter completed a set by making tea bowls to match the teapot. Here, all have been biscuit fired ready for glazing.

TIPS AND HINTS

An alternative way of making lugs is to cut circles of clay with a cutter. Then cut the circles two-thirds of the way down, and bore a hole through each.

15

15 The inside of the teapot is glazed first. Pour the glaze from a jug into the teapot, keeping your thumb over the spout. Fill it right to the top, then tip the pot upside down and pour the glaze back into the glaze bin before lifting your thumb. Blow down the spout to clear the rose. Brush glaze on the outside of the teapot with a sieving or similar brush. Clean off the base with a damp sponge. Glaze the top of the lid with a small brush, and blow through the steam hole to clear it. It is not necessary to glaze under the lid.

Basic techniques

FIRING RAKU

Some of the most exciting effects in ceramics are achieved in raku ware, and this is mainly due to the way in which raku is fired. As raku is a low-firing clay it cannot stand up to the high temperatures of conventional firing, but its open body can take the shock of rapid firing. It is possible to use a home-made kiln.

A basic raku kiln can easily be made at home from a steel drum or a frame of strong chicken wire. The insulation is provided, either inside or out, by ceramic fibre, a strong and lightweight material. The kiln is powered by propane gas and is fitted with a simple shelf. It can be stored in a shed or garage and used in your garden or yard.

Raku pots are usually decorated with plain glazes which contain oxides. There are two main reactions that produce a variety of effects — reduction and oxidation. Reduction occurs when a pot is starved of oxygen — for example, when a smouldering pot is taken straight from the kiln and placed in a metal bin or buried in sawdust. The fire loses its supply of oxygen and therefore takes it from the metals in the glaze or the clay, giving a metallic lustre to the pot. Oxidation occurs when the pot is in a clean atmosphere with oxygen . No oxygen is taken from the metal oxide so the glaze colour remains.

If you are not happy with the result of your raku firing just put the pot back into the kiln. It can be refired and reduced or oxidized repeatedly. Raku firing gives very unpredictable effects, and is part of the fun and surprise of raku — each pot is unique.

A word of warning — you should wear protective clothing and take great care throughout the whole process. Raku kilns are fired to about 1000°C (1830°F) and while taking the pots out of the kiln due care and attention should be taken.

1

1 A home-made raku kiln, consisting of ceramic fibre blanket wrapped around a former and protected by a wire mesh. The lid is insulated in the same way. The kiln is powered by propane gas and lit with a blow torch. You can make a kiln like this for your garden or yard and your local potter's supplier will give you advice on the use and availability of materials. The first firing in the kiln at each session is slow because the pots inside are cold. Place the next pots to be fired on top so that they are not completely cold when they go into the kiln. The kiln will reach a temperature of about 1000°C (1830°F), but as there is no temperature gauge this is not an accurate measurement. With experience you will be able to tell by looking when the pots are ready.

2 In the firing process the colour of the pots changes from black to red to orange. When they are ready they are a bright, glowing orange. Take great care looking into the kiln, and do not remove the lid until you are going to take out the pots. Look through the hole in the side of the kiln. If you have difficulty in seeing if the pots are ready use a torch — you will see them shine and glisten.

3

3 You should wear protective clothing and take great care throughout the whole process. Use gloves and tongs to remove the pots from the kiln, and wear a face mask to avoid inhaling harmful smoke and fumes. Here the potter has taken the teapot from the kiln and is placing it in a metal bin. There is a cushion of sawdust chips at the bottom of the bin as some protection for the pot. The pot is then covered with sawdust chips. The lid is placed on the bin to remove the source of oxygen and 'reduce' the glazing. Just before the pot is ready check for any bubbles on the surface. These will also reduce if you leave the pot in the bin for a short while.

4

4 Sawdust chippings are poured on to these tea bowls to bury them, removing the source of oxygen for reduction. Use hardwood sawdust if you can — softwood contains too much resin which produces tar and would stain your pots. If you do not want the process of reduction to take place allow the pots to burn freely taking oxygen from the air, or quench them in cold water directly after taking them from the kiln.

5 The teapot is a glowing orange colour as it is transferred from the kiln to the metal bin and the sawdust chippings catch fire from the heat of the pot. The lid is placed on the bin for about 15-20 minutes to remove the source of the oxygen while reduction takes place.

5

6

6 The smouldering teapot is removed from the bin with a pair of tongs. It is extremely hot and burning sawdust adheres to it. With experience you will have some idea of what the finished glazed effect will look like, but nothing is certain in raku firing and you may be in for a surprise. If you do not like it you can always put it back into the kiln and try again.

7

7 The pot is quenched in water and the reduction process comes to a stop. Some of the burnt sawdust comes off immediately but the rest will have to be scrubbed away.

8

8 The teapot is cleaned with wire wool to reveal the effects of the reduction on the white crackle glaze. Really scrub it well to get off all the dirt — you will not harm the pot by doing so. When it is clean and dry attach a cane handle — these are readily available from most potter's suppliers.

9 The teapot, a tea bowl, and slab dishes. The reduction on the turquoise glaze has produced a lustrous metallic glint on the dishes. Decoration can also be added by painting oxides on to the glaze, though you may not be able to plan a precise design as raku firing is so unpredictable.

Glaze recipes

Raku glaze base
Soft borax frit	45%
Standard alkaline frit	45%
China clay	5%
Bentonite	5%

for green add
Copper carbonate	4%
Tin oxide	2%

for blue add
Cobalt carbonate	2%

Crackle white glaze
Calcium borate frit	40%
Standard black frit	40%
China clay	10%
Bentonite	5%
Tin oxide	5%

Index

Acknowledgements

The authors and publishers would like special thanks to go to photographer John Melville for all his hard work and dedication, with thanks also going to Mike Bailey, Kate Mills, Steve Mills and Paul Stubbs at Bath Potters' Supplies for their advice, help and hospitality and Potclays Limited of Stoke-on-Trent for the photograph of the kilns on page 34.

Dedication

For Jay Sanderson, the Yabuuchi family of Japan and my own dear family.

Sara Pearch